BIG
BRAND
THEORY

GINGKO PRESS

BIG BRAND THEORY

ISBN 978-1-58423-445-6

First Published in the United States of America by Gingko Press
by arrangement with Sandu Publishing Co., Limited

Gingko Press, Inc.
1321 Fifth Street
Berkeley, CA 94710 USA
Tel: (510) 898 1195
Fax: (510) 898 1196
Email: books@gingkopress.com
www.gingkopress.com

Sponsored by: Design 360° – Concept and Design Magazine
Chief Editor: Wang Shaoqiang
Executive Editor: Krystle Zhang
Chief Designer: Wang Shaoqiang
Book Designer: Ginger Lau
Sales Managers:
Niu Guanghui (China), Daniela Huang (International)
Address:
3rd Floor, West Tower,
No.10 Ligang Road, Haizhu District,
510280, Guangzhou, China
Tel: (86)-20-84344460
Fax: (86)-20-84344460
sandu.sales@gmail.com
www.sandu360.com

Printed and bound in China

CONTENTS

FOREWORD

TIE ME UP, TIE ME DOWN

by Ian Lynam, Graphic Designer and Writer

The absolute pinnacle of my father's adventures in fashion in the later years of his career was a series of neckties whose graphic anti-patterns were designed by Grateful Dead bandleader Jerry Garcia. This was highly anachronistic in that my dad's musical taste leans toward opera singer Luciano Pavarotti, not hippy jam bands. Not to denigrate my father (or his fashion sense), but it makes sense that the lone arena of fashion in which he, a real estate analyst for The State of New York then working in the state's bland capitol and its miles of modular cubicles, would be his neckties. Garcia's hallucinogenic spatters could easily be mistaken for old British marbling patterns, or would lend the wearer cool "outsider" status if the nature of the graphics were questioned, though I'm sure my dad would be quick to quip his own facetious comment at the expense of Herr Garcia were he questioned at length about the nature of his neckwear in the office.[1]

This brings up some interesting ideas about style, authenticity and quality. While my dad was rocking some stylish[2] neckties, they weren't necessarily true to who he as a person is. In the book The Substance of Style by Virginia Postrel[3] there are some compelling inquiries into the value of authenticity. Authenticity is dissected as having multiple definitions springing from the original (though thoroughly impersonal) definition of the term: purity of intention, ethnic identity, applied legitimacy, tradition, the patina of age versus replicas, and authenticity as a "rhetorical club to enforce the critic's taste". A secondary, more individualized, and more democratic version of authenticity is suggested: an authenticity that is self-serving and subjective, providing formal pleasure, connections to history and tradition, and propping up self-expression as being ultimately "authentic".

That something is authentic is theoretically valuable, but what if the subject in question is authentic but of little aesthetic value or has a minimum of craft and focus on the part of the maker(s)? To be real is fine, but what if an object or person is both authentic and crappy? The world is full of authentic designed objects that provide truly foul real-world experiences. Try sitting on an Eames bucket chair (or an Aeron chair for that matter) and actually working for more than two hours. These "design objects" are sought-after artifacts for their aesthetic qualities, but they'll provide singularly uncomfortable sitting experiences.

This juxtaposition of authenticity and quality is something that I have come back to often over the past few years. I've found brand strategy that evaluates both sides of the coin (aesthetics and information) to be an increasing aspect of my own professional practice, making me a planner/advisor just as much as a graphic designer. It's an interesting place to be - innate core values being decided hand-in-hand with aesthetics. It's what design can be - a pluralistic way of assessing and providing form-giving to objects of desire from a holistic perspective.

And this is where branding comes in: brands are so much bigger than logos, type choices, color palettes and packaging designs. Most brand-oriented books published by design media focus solely on the facades applied to contemporary brands, but just as important are the products contained within. Branding is such a totalizing force: the manipulation of desire through tugging at all-too-human aspirations, comforts, trusts, vanity and a gamut of other feelings. For most brands, things fall flat somewhere – be it massive big box retailers' destruction of local economies, footwear companies' labor issues or web browser developers' late-to-the-

Ian Lynam is a graphic designer and writer living in Tokyo. He runs a multidisciplinary design studio that focuses on pan-cultural identity design, motion graphics, and editorial design. He is a graduate of Portland State University (B.S. Graphic Design) and California Institute of the Arts (M.F.A. Graphic Design). His most recent book is Design of Manga, Anime & Light Novels. An Asia Pacific Design Award winner, he writes regularly for Idea Magazine, Slanted Magazine, Néojaponisme, and a host of design books.

More: ianlynam.com

game attention to design detail. Branding strategists want consumers to think of brands as entities with which to interact with, yet act blissfully unaware that the dewey-eyed multinational corporation with the glossy sheen in fact is an advocate of child labor or savage mining of rare resources whose products fall apart as quickly as they were manufactured.

In this peculiar moment of graphic design and the near-collective obsession with easy solutions masquerading as critical practice[4] in more academic design circles, thinking bigger and assessing structure and content in a truly considered, craft-centric fashion is the least we should do, both as designers and as brands. Taste and style are great, but they are not nearly enough in how we assess clients or client design options[5]. If we interacted with others merely because we spoke the same cultural shorthand[6], we wouldn't get very far... and they'd never criticize our choice of neckwear.

[1] Interestingly, this Dead-inspired fashion coincided with a spate of appearances in Albany by the Grateful ones themselves. Around this time, my long-locked, heavy metal enthusiast younger brother procured an Albany Police badge from a garage sale and took to cruising Grateful Dead show parking lots, shaking down hippies for their drugs and letting them off with "just a warning", keeping the goods for our consumption.

[2] "Stylish" here meaning "imbued with style", not necessarily something I'd wear.

[3] One of those pop criticism books that is an interesting hybrid experience – part historical synthesis, part analysis of contemporary trends (or, more appropriately, then – contemporary trends, as it was published in 2004), and an aggregate of opinions on general cultural trending toward an acceptance of aesthetic pluralism. It's one of those "important" books that has flown under the radar lately due to a less than timeless cover design, some of the ideas within having been espoused by others both prior to and after publication, and an apparent lack of widespread recognition beyond its time as a New York Times Notable Book selection. That being said, it is one of the few must-read books of aesthetic criticism due to it's target: design, surface and the everyday.

[4] And just as popular fascination with simplistic "Modern" aesthetics.

[5] Please note the use of the word "options" in lieu of "solutions". The term "design solution" is design propaganda – no "solution" ever exists – there is always something slicker around the corner.

[6] If each of your friends all liked exactly the same music, fashion, books and cultural ephemera, you'd probably get pretty bored pretty quickly.

Ian Lynam

FOREWORD

BIG BRAND THEORY

by Jesper von Wieding, Strategic Creative Director
and co-founder of 3X.dk

It a great honour for me to be asked to write the preface for this book – BIG BRAND THEORY!

As a strategic creative designer I have over the years spent big part of my professional career working with national and international well-known company and product brands.

An important part of our daily life, as designers, is to keep updating ourselves on the daily life around us, new lifestyles, trends or movements. Many designers search for inspiration using the internet and some of us just can't live without these moments - visiting design bookstores! No matter where I am in the world I just have to pass by a bookstore! It has become a habit that I can't live without. I am addicted - I need my monthly dose and can't live without it! These soundless moments are fantastic, when I find myself, in the company with a good friend or alone, completely relaxed and surrounded by books and other readers. I can't get enough looking at design books, featuring spectacular "best of" compilations with "Case studies" of the high-profiled branding campaigns, providing invaluable sources of inspiration and knowledge, guiding us to understand the key elements of their successful brand or design.

So what is a brand?

Many would define a brand as a name, term, design, symbol, or any other feature that identifies one seller's good or service as distinct from those of other sellers. The legal term for brand is trademark. It's interesting to look back in the history because the word branding originally means a way to tell one person's cattle from another by the use of a hot stamp iron. Today branding is also about positive perception, customer loyalty, excess price, it's a recruitment tool and a valuable asset for the company that owns it.

"The days of 'hidden' companies are way over..."

No big international companies or organizations can survive and lead a market today up against their competitors, without a clear understanding and full control of their own corporate and/or product brand identity!

Jesper von Wieding has over his 25 years of graphic design experience within Corporate Identity, Brand Development, Packaging Design, Fashion / lifestyle, furniture design, exhibition design and interior design. He has worked in USA, France, Germany, Stockholm, Oslo and Copenhagen. He is one of the founders and former co-partner of Scandinavian DesignLab. In 2010, Jesper left Scandinavian DesignLab to pursue new challenges by establishing the company 3X (www.3X.dk), a company of strategic creative consultant's & entrepreneurs. 3X is a company with a unique combination of expertise that spans from art, culture, design, branding, entertainment, education, publishing to food and beverage. 3X has offices in Beijing, Copenhagen, Guangzhou, Hong Kong China and Kuala Lumpur.

A brand is the visual extract of the identity!

When developing a new brand identity it's therefore important that the relationship between the design agency and their client is build on sharing, insight, knowledge and trust! No Big Brand identity is developed without an in-depth understanding of the client's vision (Out of reach – but within sight!), mission (How do we get there?), strategy, values (difficult to copy and relevant to the customers/target groups) and that differentiates the company from its competitors (Point of difference / POD).

"Think forward stay forward."

The fashion industry is well-known for being fast and unpredictable. Working as a graphic designer within the fashion industry requires the ability to transform emotional values into strong visual concepts and constantly to be able to capture and interpret new trends, constantly being able to challenge, develop and create new visual expressions combining different materials and new printing techniques. This book shows examples of that and very much more across media!

I hope that you will enjoy reading BIG BRAND THEORY. The case stories that you will find in the book span from living, food & drink, fashion, culture, exhibition to promotion! I am sure that you will experience design work developed by "some of the best in class". This book will show some of the latest brands boom in the market economy and the secrets why classic brands live long in people's mind as well. I hope that you will find just the inspiration you are looking for.

I wish you good luck!

LIFESTYLE GOODS & SERVICES

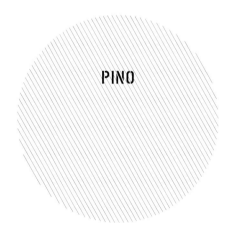

Project _ PINO
Design Agency _ Bond Creative Agency
Creative Direction _ Jesper Bange, Aleksi Hautamaki
Photography _ Paavo Lehtonen
Client _ PINO

The store concept for interior decoration shop Pino is based on its name, which means a "pile" or a "stack" in Finnish. That is taken visually into the new logo and the design of the shop fixtures. The interior design concept, with its subtle palette, works as a neutral background for the fresh, colourful visual identity and products.

Project _ C - Convenience with Care
Design Agency _ e-Types
Design _ Andreas Peitersen, Jess Andersen, Jonas Hecksher
Strategy _ Mari Lea Randsborg, Michael Thouber
Client _ COOP Denmark

Building on Coop's heritage, e-Types helped define a concept that modernized the ideals inherent in Coop's co-op tradition - a tradition that hails back to 1886 when Pastor H.C Sonne launched Denmark's first consumer cooperative. Today C offers expanded opening hours to suit the busy work life of modern families, ethically sourced goods, and lifestyle products as well as healthy take away - alongside cheap day-to-day items recognizing that while we will gladly pay a premium for that bio-dynamic Barolo, we feel slightly more ambiguous when it comes to toilet paper and tooth brushes. e-Types developed the name, logo, and identity for C - reinterpreting Coop´s original values into a heart. The logo signals the care for people's health and economy as well as the concern for the world around us that lie at the very core of Coop.

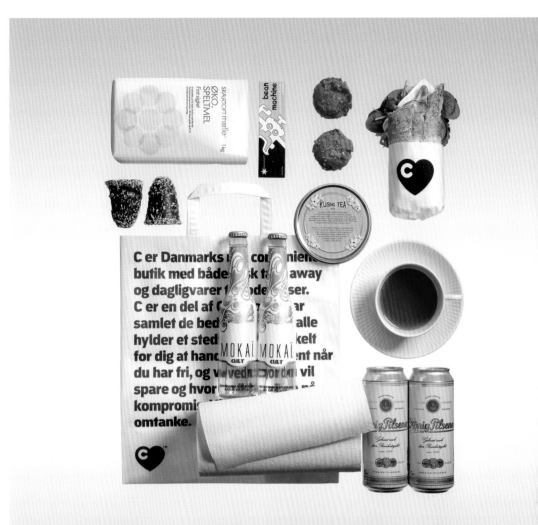

IM9OSSIBLE

Project _ New Corporate Design for Impossible
Design Agency _ Heine / Lenz / Zizka Projekte GmbH
Design _ Heine / Lenz / Zizka
Client _ Impossible

The mastermind of the new identity and design of all Impossible products and activities is the design agency Heine / Lenz / Zizka in Berlin. The Corporate Design emphasizes the analog quality of Impossible by clarity and haptic details. Also the nomenclature of the new films as well the packaging design was developed by Heine / Lenz / Zizka. The agency was founded in 1989 and is amongst the top 20 design agencies in Germany.

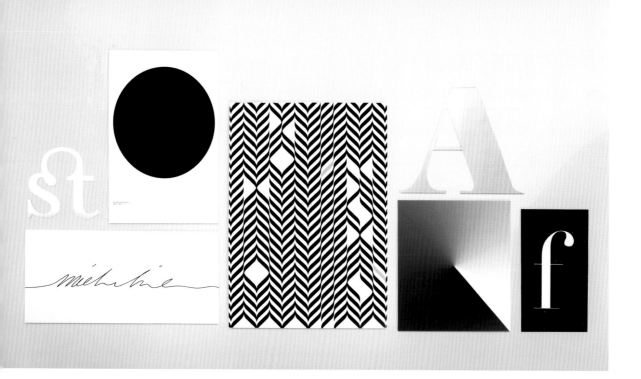

Project _ Micheline Branding
Design Agency _ Anagrama
Client _ Micheline Branding

Micheline is a print-shop boutique dedicated to designing and printing stationery and pieces for social events. Interested in rejuvenating the brand in order to captivate the unexplored segment of young adults, Micheline came to Anagrama.

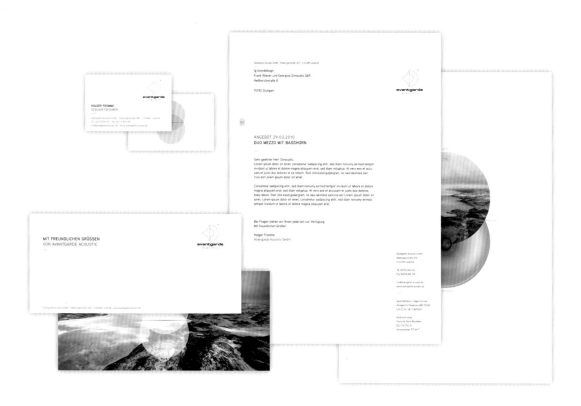

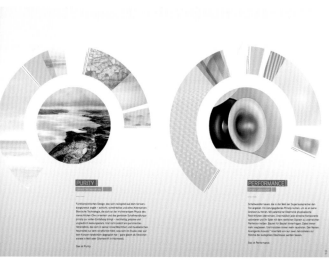

AVANTGARDE
ACOUSTIC

Project _ Avantgarde Acoustic
Design Agency _ fg branddesign
Creative Direction & Design _ Frank Rösner, Georgios
Simoudis
Client _ Avantgarde Acoustic

Avantgarde Acoustic is the worlds most renowned
manufacturer of horn loudspeakers. The overwhelming
sound experience of an Avantgarde Acoustic loudspeaker
turned the brand into the leader of the premium
audio branch within just two decades. The goal of the
cooperation with fg branddesign was to convey this high
level of quality through all means of communication.
The starting point of the collaboration was the joint
positioning workshop in which the management
participated as well as employees from product design,
sales, development and controlling. The result of
this interdisciplinary compounded workshop was the
archetypal positioning of the combined characters, the
creator and the pure. Based on that the development
of the communicational guideline "purity meets
performance" was carried out. The implementation of the
communicational guideline started off with the corporate
brochure, product brochures, a facelift of the website and
other means of communication. More recently several
videos about the company were released winning awards
such as the master of excellence award and the master
award at the International Corporate Media Festival.

Purity meets Performance
The voice of Avantgarde Acoustic

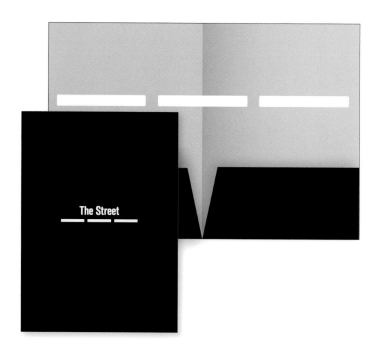

The Street

TS

MAIN ST

Stockpickr

THE STREET

Project _ The Street
Design Agency _ Pentagram Design
Design _ Paula Scher
Client _ TheStreet.com Inc

Financial media company The Street launched a new graphic identity as a part of a company-wide rebranding. As a provider of stock market analysis, The Street is authoritative, accessible, and up-to-the-minute, and the new identity is designed to be distinctive and cohesive, strengthening the brand across The Street's various sites and platforms. Set in a modified Akzidenz Grotesk, the new logotype appears above three short lines that suggest lines in the street or balance sheets. (The number of lines was inspired by the market positions of buy, sell and hold.) The identity also appears as a monogram of the letters "TS" that can be used as an icon for apps and social media like Twitter. The designers created a family of logos for the site's affiliates that all read as being part of The Street.

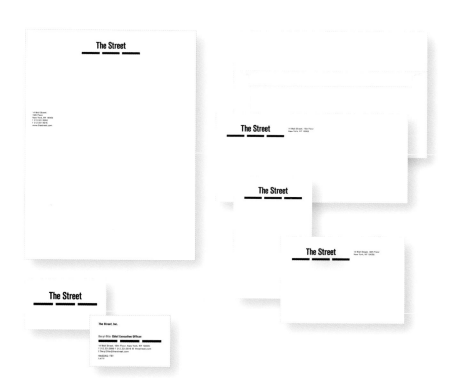

The Street

Project _ Editions of 100
Design Agency _ BERG
Design _ Daniel Freytag
Client _ Editions of 100

The Editions of 100 project came about because we were asked a number of times if we sold posters we'd designed for various clients. So we thought, why not build an online shop for ourselves, a place where we can post non commercial projects for sale to the public. The project involved creating a brand identity, suite of stationery and website. The website is a Big Cartel e-commerce CMS with a customized branded template.

NASU
GARDEN
OUTLET

Project _ NASU GARDEN OUTLET
Design Agency _ Hiromura Design Office
Art Director _ Masaaki Hiromura
Design _ Chie Nakao
Copywriter _ Fukiko Kojima
Illustration _ Tomoko Nagata
Client _ SEIBU PROPERTIES INC.

The visual identity project for NASU GARDEN OUTLET. It is the outlet center located in Nasu which is famous as a resort in Japan. The clean and elegant shopping court is located on the ground floor. This includes various 120 retails such as luxury brands, clothing stores, sports shops, cafes and restaurants, which can accept wide range of people.

NASU GARDEN
OUTLET

Project _ The People's Supermarket
Design Agency _ Unreal
Design _ Ryan Tym, Liana Zammit
Client _ The People's Supermarket

The final identity for The People's Supermarket is based on the classic retail symbol of a Euroslot (the hole punched at the top of packaged products which allows them to be hung up in shops).

The Euroslot can be easily cut through anything from letterheads to in-store packaging, creating a simple, clever and cost-effective branding device that can be consistently applied across all communications.

The completed project is friendly in its look and utilitarian in approach, being applied in a bold, straightforward manner and always appearing in two colours. The strong use of yellow represents the colour of t-shirts which members are given when they join.

K11 DesignStore

Project _ K11 Design Store Branding
Design Agency _ BLOW
Design Direction _ Ken Lo
Creative Direction _ Ken Lo
Art Direction _ Ken Lo
Design _ Ken Lo, Crystal Cheung
Client _ K11 Design Store

K11 Design Store is a new retail store in K11 Art Mall. The products are selected from outstanding designers' brands all over the world. Some brands and styles are first brought into Hong Kong China. Wandering in K11 Design Store is like visiting a design museum.

We were asked to create the whole look and feel for this new design store, from the logo, packaging, environmental graphics to promotion.

K11 DESIGN STORE

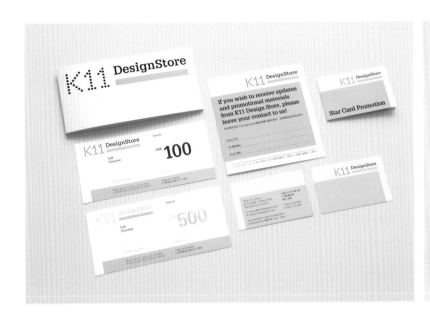

Project _ Abracadabra. Children's Books
Design Agency _ Salon de Thé
Design _ Rosa Lladó and Roser Cerdà
Client _ Abracadabra Bookstore

The name of Abracadabra's bookstore is a magic word from the Arabian Nights stories. Really is a special word: it has 5 vowels, and all are "A", and the A is as door, a door to a magic world: a children's bookstore with special and beautiful books.

The logo design uses simple geometric shapes inspired in children's games. We also like a non-static logo. We played with the letters building different forms, but, anyway we wanted it to be always recognizable. We chose a bright colour – fluorescent pink – to identify it; we didn't want to use typical primary colours usually applied to children's toys: red, yellow, green and blue. We also designed some signs – a pram – using the structure of the letters.

For the bookstore's signage we also chose another colour – a green-blue colour – which helps to separate different shelves that contain books distributed by age. This bookstore is different from others because it has books in different languages. We advertise this through cloud-labels on the shop window. We designed elements for comunication: an sticker to seal bags and to use on the wrapping; bookshop business cards, postcards, and a cloth bag for the store's birthday celebration.

Project _ D100 Idenity
Design Agency _ Mind Design
Creative Direction _ Holger Jacobs
Art Direction _ Craig Sinnamon
Client _ D100 Dentistry

D100 is a modern dentistry at the Barbican (100 Aldersgate street). The identity is inspired by the raking patterns around stones in Japanese Zen gardens and protective layers of enamel around teeth. The pattern have also been applied to the interior going around furniture and various fixed or removable object in the practice.

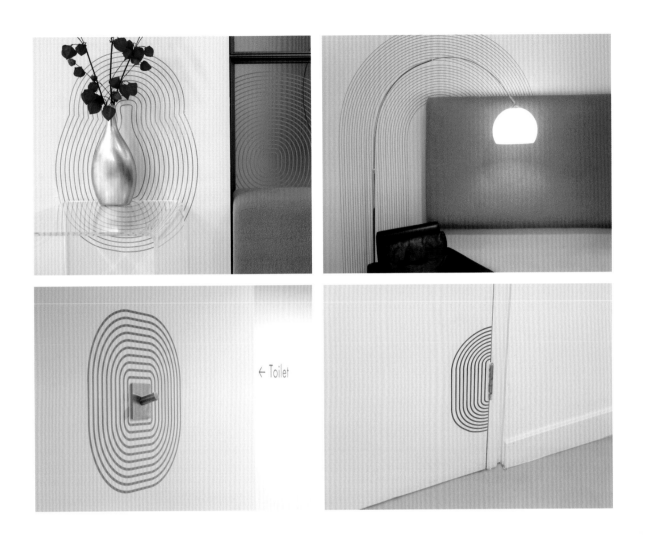

← Toilet

031

Project _ DOWIN
Design Agency _ Linshaobin Design
Design _ Lin Shaobin, Ma Xiaoqin, Lin Chun, Peng Feng
Client _ Multibiolog Personal Care Products Co,.Ltd

DOWIN roots in Korean fashion culture with twenty years' history. It's a company dedicated to personal care products for 80's and 90's. Its marketing network covers Mainland China, Hong Kong China, Korea and other regions.

DOWIN

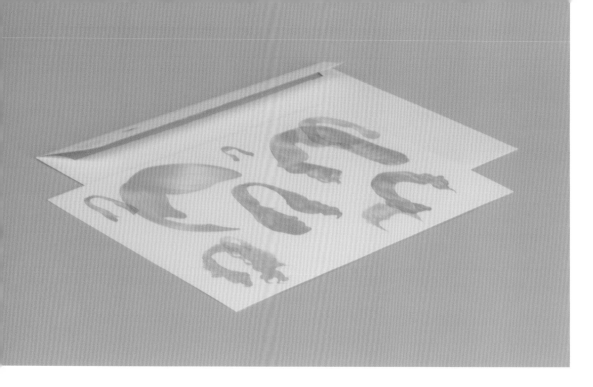

Project _ Zenzero
Design _ Alfio Mazzei
Client _ Zenzero

Zenzero is a beauty salon in Lugano, Switzerland. The client request was an elegant visual identity which gave the right look to the activity.

The Idea behind the logo is an haircut in an explicit and simple way. The chosen colour represent the Ginger root, because Zenzero in Italian means Ginger.

The invitation for the opening plays with the logo concept, but using a coloured collage of haircuts, some of which belong to a famous person.

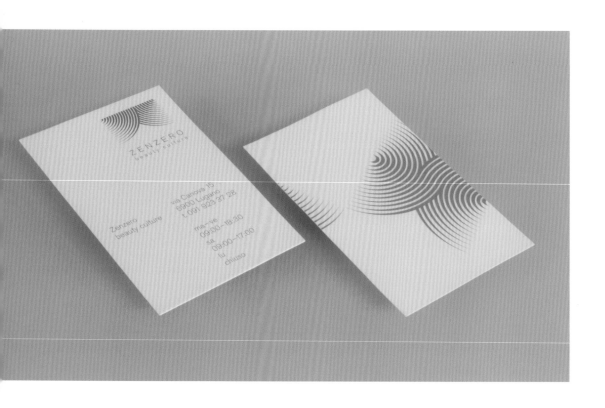

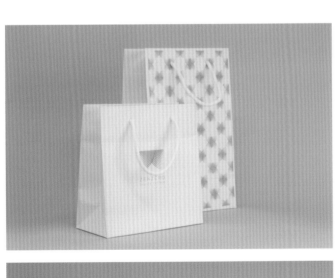

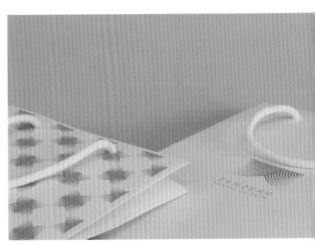

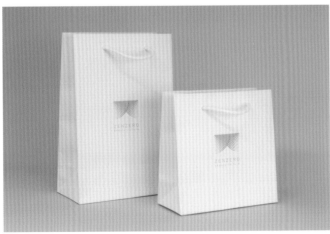

GEM MODELS

Project _ GEM Models Identity
Design Agency _ kissmiklos
Design _ Miklós Kiss
Photography _ identity photos : Miklós Kiss, models photos : Orsolya Hajas
Client _ GEM Models

Identity and web design for a new model agency. The logo reflects the meaning of the word gem. I tried to design a very characteristic, a very fashionable and interesting logo, so I redesigned a typical blackletter script.

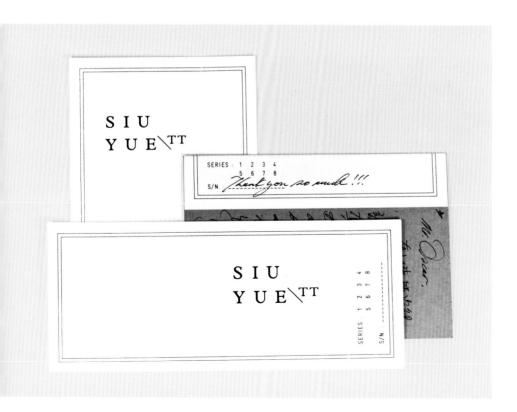

SIUYUETT

Project _ SiuYuett
Design _ Idea With Legs
Client _ SiuYuett

An Identity for a book-binding artist's own brand - SiuYuett.

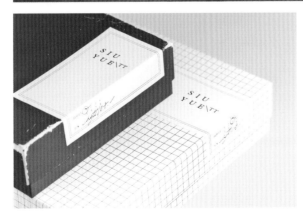

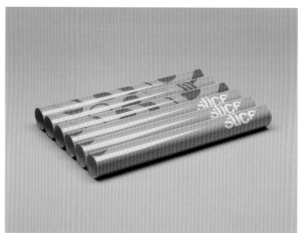

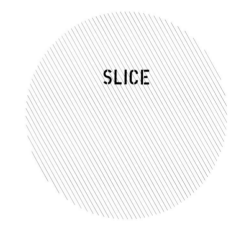

Project _ Slice
Design Agency _ Manual
Creative Direction _ Tom Crabtree
Design _ Tom Crabtree, Eileen Lee, Joshua Swanbeck
Illustration _ Joshua Swanbeck, Eileen Lee
Client _ Slice

Slice collaborates with world-renowned designers to create award-winning innovative cutting tools. The identity is based upon a simple graphic gesture that is employed consistently throughout all print and packaging aspects of the brand.

By simply cutting into the word "slice" the logo that instantly communicates the nature of the company and its products. This sliced angle becomes and integral part of the packaging system, often being used in interesting architectural ways, to reveal typographic information and to add a physical branding element to the structures.

SLICE

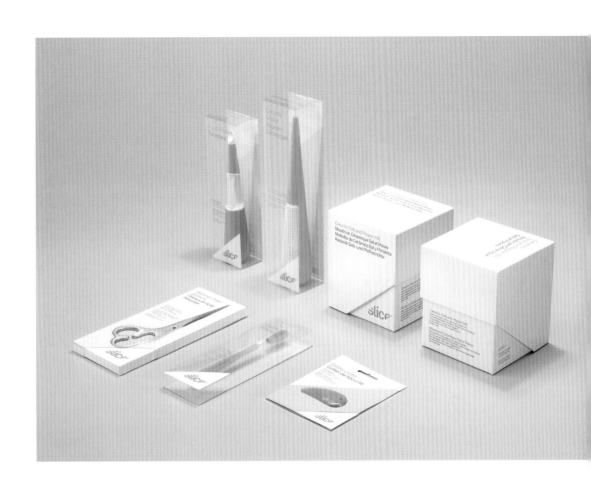

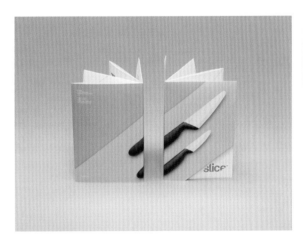

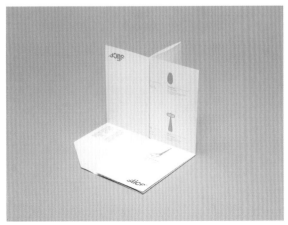

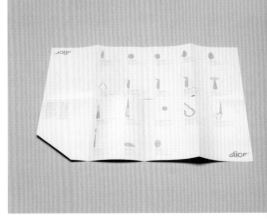

Project _ IDEA EXPRESS
Design Agency _ Studiowill
Client _ IDEA EXPRESS

Idea Express is a new Hong Kong China based company which creates beautifully designed accessories exclusively for Apple computers.

We created a logo that combined the capital letters "I" and "E".

A customized font was used to enhance the brand's characteristic.

It embodies the form of the letter "I" distorted through high speed motion, whilst taking on the form of an abstract letter "E", creating a monogram which fuses the company's initials.

The simple and environmentally friendly packaging range we developed for Idea Express provides a flexible system and range of materials that can be adapted to suit the ever changing needs of the sales business.

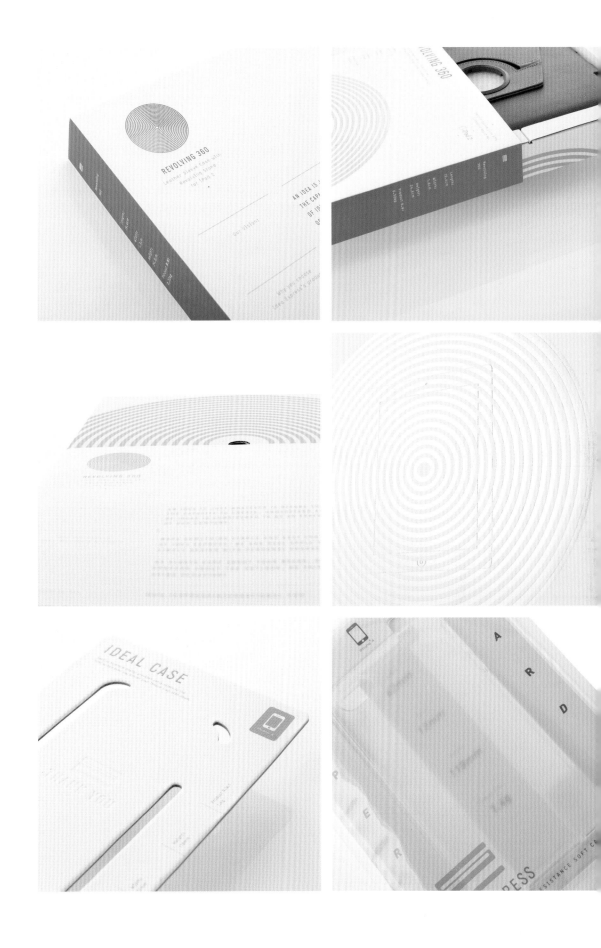

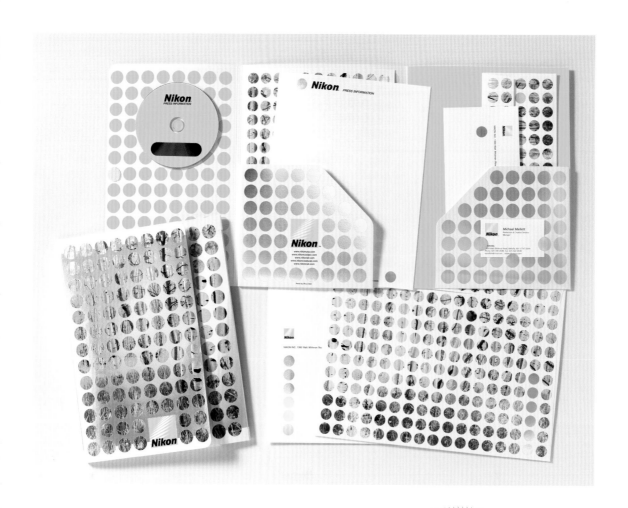

Project _ Nikon Digital
Design Agency _ Mirko Ilic Corp.
Creative Direction _ Mirko Ilic
Art Direction _ Michael Mellett
Design _ Mirko Ilic
Client _ Nikon Digital

Nikon Digital press kit & direct mail.

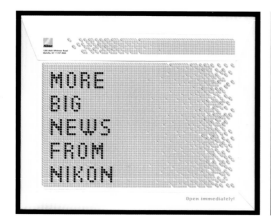

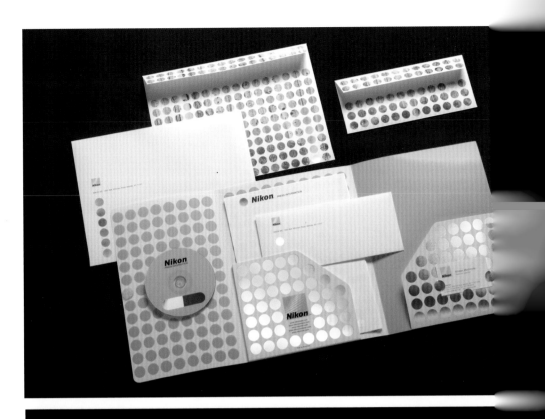

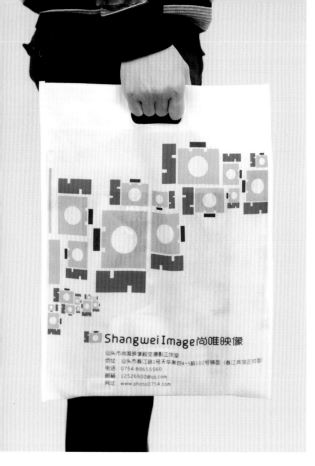

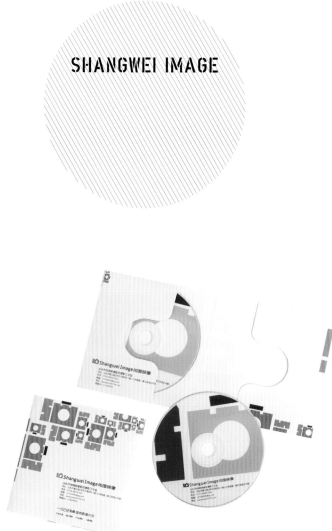

SHANGWEI IMAGE

Project _ Shangwei Image
Design Agency _ Linshaobin Design
Design _ Lin Shaobin, Ma Xiaoqin, Chen Xiaoqiang
Client _ Shangwei Image

Shangwei is a photography studio for figure portraits and wedding photographs. We designed a camera form by the English letters of Shangwei as the core brand image.

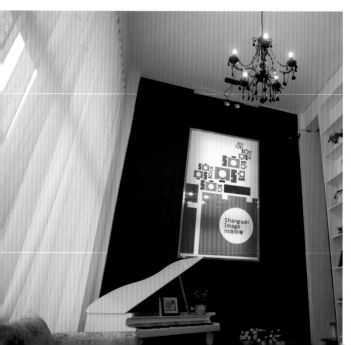

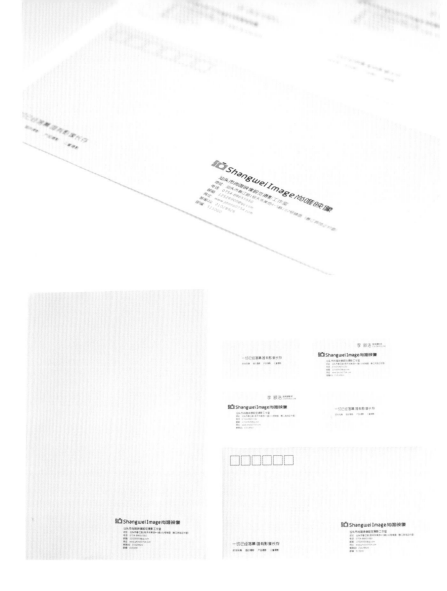

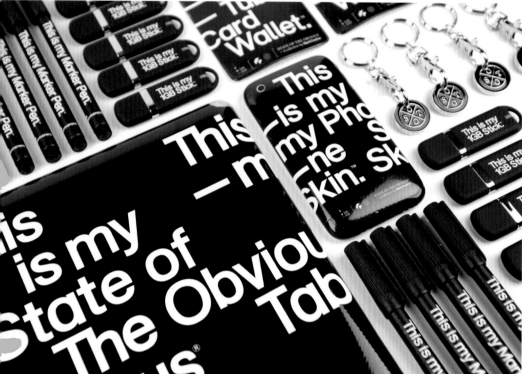

Project _ Design Museum x State of the Obvious® Collection
Design Agency _ Mash Creative
Design _ Mash Creative
Client _ Design Museum x State of the Obvious®

Extending the philosophy & thinking behind our branded State of the Obvious® collection, we have designed a set of products exclusively for the Design Museum.

The design of these products has been heavily influenced by the International Typographic Style from the 50's and 60's & shows an evolution from our original S/O/T/O collection. It has been designed to appeal to typography and design lovers alike.

At S/O/T/O we design and produce products which not only look good but also have a useful function. The exclusive Design Museum collection consists of iPhone 3 & 4 and iPad 1 & 2 GelaSkins, Staedtler Marker Pens, USB Sticks, Travel Card Wallets and Keyrings.

DESIGN MUSEUM
x STATE OF THE
OBVIOUS®

STATE OF
THE OBVIOUS®
COLLECTION

Project _ State of the Obvious® Collection
Design Agency _ Mash Creative
Design _ Mash Creative
Client _ Mash Creative

With consumerism at an all time high and brand image playing an ever more important role in consumers buying choices, we felt an overwhelming desire to challenge what has become "The Norm".

At Mash Creative we believe there is a niche in the market for a collection of products which turns conventional branding on its head. S/O/T/O (State of the Obvious) is a range of merchandise and apparel which does just that. S/O/T/O uses the products description to create a unique brand identity.

The S/O/T/O collection is designed to have a playful, modern and bold brand image which is flexible enough to be adapted across a wide variety of items. The collection will continue to grow with many other products already in the pipeline.com

Project _ Fahrschule Elbs Corporate Identity Redesign
Design Agency _ FORMZOO
Design _ Markus Guenther
Credits _ Lars Erbach, Sebastian Herrlinger, Robert Zirk
Client _ Fahrschule Elbs

In spring 2009 our friends of the south German driving school ELBS asked us, if we had some ideas to improve their appearance. The client gave us free hand on the job and within the next month we developed this highly illustrative and non-typical corporate design. The design includes logo, business cards stationary, corporate design manual and the website.

ELBS
DIE FAHRSCHULE

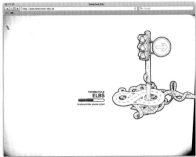

ELBS
DIE FAHRSCHULE

Ansgar und Charly Elbs

In Ulm und Laupheim   www.fahrschule-elbs.de
Tel. 0172 / 28 32 429   info@fahrschule-elbs.de

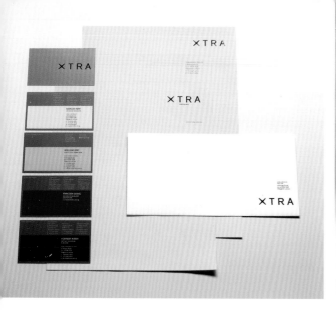

Project _ XTRA Corporate Identity
Design Agency _ &Larry
Design _ Larry Peh
Client _ XTRA

The rebranding for one of Singapore's foremost retailers of designer furnishings began its logotype. The old arrangement of "XTRA" was simplified, capitalized and spaced out to achieve a clean and timeless presentation. The distinctive "XTRA" draws its strength and inspiration from cross-sections found in classic designs like the Eames La Chaise. Thicker at the centre and tapered at the ends, the "XTRA" appears strong yet elegant, creating a focal point and differentiating itself from modern typefaces. The new identity includes stationery and name cards, all designed to project a tasteful and serious persona to customers and business partners.

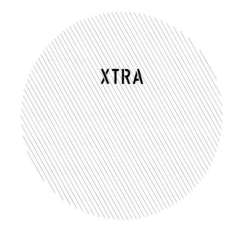

Project _ Jagad Furniture
Design Agency _ Bobchen Design Office Hangzhou
Design _ Bob Chen
Client _ Jagad Furniture Store

Founded in 2008, Jagad Furniture was exclusive sales of Southeast Asia furniture. The style is rustic, primitive and modern. Its store emphasizes "non-mass-produced," "diversity" and "original". The purpose is not to sell products, but also deal with the interpersonal feelings in daily life.

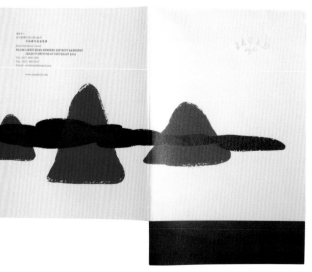

TOUCH FEELING

TOUCH FEELING
FURNITURE

Project _ Touch Feeling Furniture
Design Agency _ Bobchen Design Office Hangzhou
Design _ Bob Chen
Client _ Touch Feeling Furniture Brand

The materials of Touch Feeling Furniture is the high-quality teak from Indonesia. The designer created a classic prototype to reflect the life attitude of "Touch Feeling" by the consideration of touch, scale, technology, vision, time and quality.

BELMACZ

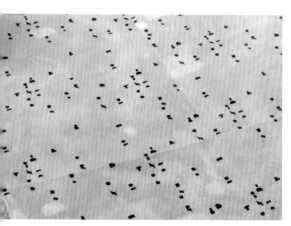

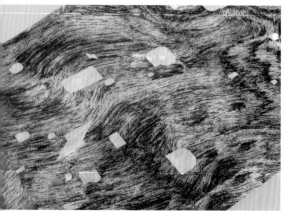

Project _ Belmacz Identity
Design _ Mind Design
Client _ Belmacz

Belmacz is a London based jewelry company who will open its first shop and gallery in London Mayfair soon. For this reason we have re-designed the original identity and worked in collaboration with Jump Studios on the interior.

The new identity takes the original logo (which has been in use for about 8 years) but adds a variety of thicker, "raw" letter shapes. Those shapes relate to the process in which raw minerals and diamonds are more and more refined until they become a piece of jewelry. The visual references start with the mines, go to the raw materials, the raw letter shapes and in the end to the refined letter shapes of the original logo.

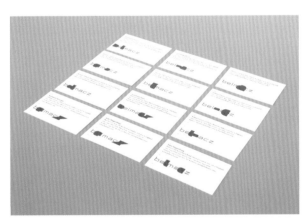

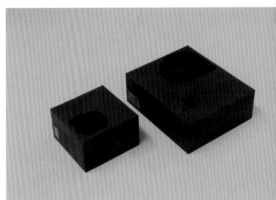

SIX SCENTS PARFUMS

Project _ Six Scents Fragrance Initiative
Design Agency_ 3 Deep Design
Art direction _ 3 Deep Design
Design _ 3 Deep Design
Client _ Six Scents Parfums

What if a fragrance could be more than just sensuality, intrigue and allure? What if it could represent something that you stand for, something you believe in and hope for? Introducing The Six Scents Global Fragrance Initiative.

Annually, a distinct group of six prominent artists and perfumers are selected to develop a limited edition series of fragrances to help raise money for charity. The collection represents a worldwide spectrum of contemporary perspectives on creativity and culture.

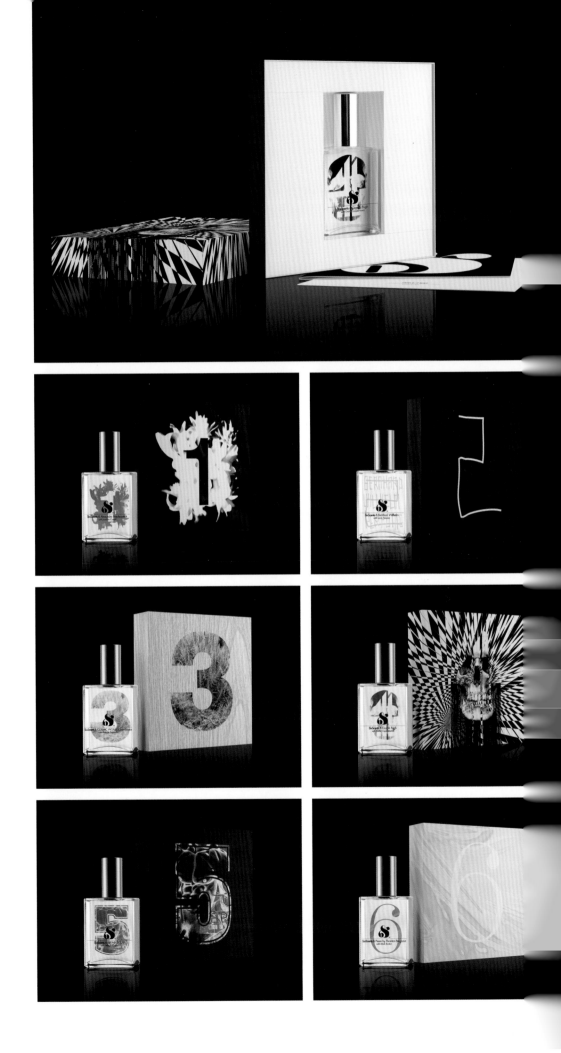

Project _ Hotel Ambrose Identity and Wine Selection Label
Design Agency _ kissmiklos and imprvd
Design _ Miklós Kiss
Photography _ Miklós Kiss

Ambrose is a little hotel in Montreal. The hotel occupies II. Victorian style buildings, built in 1910. I wanted to design a logotype, which is classic like Victorian style but fresh. Firstly I was looking for II. Victorian style letters, and I studied the characters styles. After I started to draw by hand. When I developed the final form, I scanned that. And I started to refine the line, and the style. After all, I was looking for a suitable font, that to develop the typographic system. This font is a Titillium. Many places I cut the logotype, and I think therefore became fresher, and more stylish. And the contrast between the logotype script style and the complementary font san serif style are very nice single unit. I tried to expand the basis identity and I made some other concepts for example Wine Label, Clean Room Please Card, Room Numbers, Floor Information Tables...etc.

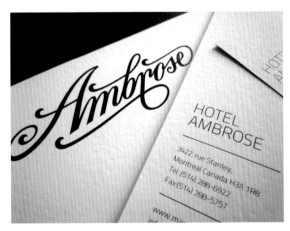

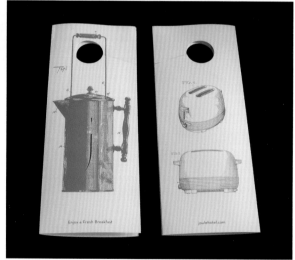

THE JOULE HOTEL

Project _ The Joule Hotel
Design Agency _ Mirko Ilic Corp.
Creative Direction _ Mirko Ilic
Art Direction _ Mirko Ilic
Design _ Jee-eun Lee, Mirko Ilic
Client _ The Joule Hotel

Identity, signage, and collateral design
for the Joule Hotel in Dallas, Texas.

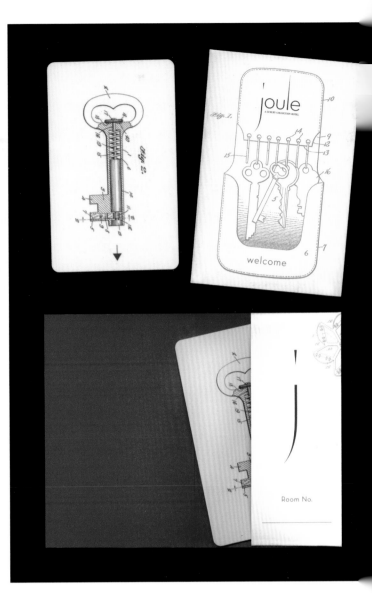

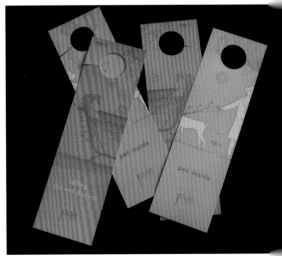

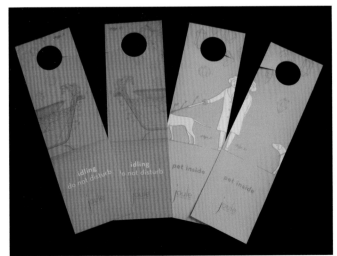

FOOD & DRINK

BAKER'S 12

Project _ Baker's 12
Design Agency _ Shenkar College of Engineering and Design
Instructor _ Nurit Koniak
Design _ Enav Tomer
Client _ Baker's 12

Baker's Dozen, is an urban lighthearted pastry shop, using naive illustrations and humorous phrases.

MELT CHOCOLATE

Project _ Melt Chocolate
Design Agency _ JJAAKK
Design _ Jesse Kirsch
Client _ Melt

Packaging and logo design for a gourmet chocolate shop. The characteristics of melted chocolate are used in an unexpected and sophisticated way reinforcing the wonderfulness contained within.

melt

melt Dark Chocolate Covered Pecans

melt Milk Chocolate Covered Almonds

melt Milk Chocolate Covered Cashews

Project _ bon doux KINOKUNIYA
Design Agency _ Hiromura Design Office
Art Director _ Masaaki Hiromura
Design _ Chie Nakao
Copywriter _ Hiroshi Mitsui
Client _ KINOKUNIYA Co.,Ltd.

The visual identity and package design project for an original chocolate brand of KINOKUNIYA, a traditional supermarket chain in Tokyo.

bon doux
KINOKUNIYA

BON DOUX
KINOKUNIYA

Project _ Brooklyn Fare
Design Agency _ Mucca Design and Design
Copywriters _ Andrea Brown, Steven Jockisch, Darren Farrell
Photography _ Hana Nakamura, Luca Pioltelli
Client _ Brooklyn Fare

While waiting to order at Brooklyn Fare's café, customers are greeted by the wide menu dangling above the counter, which reads, "We don't mind if you look us up and down." This local spot, which serves as neighborhood market, 4-star kitchen and café is rife with witty phrases that appear on everything from take-out containers to the T-shirts and aprons worn by staff. Brown paper napkins instruct patrons to "Wipe that smile on your face," to-go coffee cups read "It's a small not a tall," and brown paper shopping bags let customers know, "We like to get carried away with food." Brooklyn Fare's branding image is clever, yet simplistic. One customized font appears with four standard colours throughout the store with the purpose of creating accessible and friendly focal points for customers in a busy space brimming with locals seeking gourmet groceries and delicious, prepared meals.

Our roots are in
Brooklyn, and in
the produce section.

Joseph Lobello
Produce Manager
Joseph@BrooklynFare.com

Brooklyn Fare

200 Schermerhorn St.
Brooklyn, NY 11201
T (718) 243-0050
F (718) 243-0926

Brooklyn Fare

Our market won't
drain your savings.

Richard Lowell
General Manager
Richard@BrooklynFare.com

Brooklyn Fare

200 Schermerhorn St.
Brooklyn, NY 11201
T (718) 243-0050
F (718) 243-0926

Brooklyn Fare

Rarely is service
this well-done.

Vinnie Festa
Butcher
Vinnie@BrooklynFare.com

Brooklyn Fare

200 Schermerhorn St.
Brooklyn, NY 11201
T (718) 243-0050
F (718) 243-0926

Brooklyn Fare

BrooklynFare.com

A letter-perfect
selection of
fine foods.

200 Schermerhorn St.
Brooklyn, NY 11201
T (718) 243-0050
F (718) 243-0926

**Wipe that smile
on your face.**

BrooklynFare.com

200 Schermerhorn St.
Brooklyn, NY, 11201

Brooklyn Fare

Carry
the day...
and the
groceries.

BrooklynFare.com

We're
ready
for you to
take
us out.

fresh prepared foods
BrooklynFare.com

We carry
the stuff
you need.

fine foods & more
BrooklynFare.com

We like
to get
carried
away
with food.

fine foods & more
BrooklynFare.com

Project _ DRY Soda
Design Agency _ Turnstyle
Design _ Steven Watson
Client _ DRY Soda

DRY Soda produces less sweet, all natural, culinary sodas. Bold, colorful, graphic illustrations communicate DRY's distinctive flavors. Clear bottles allow the purity of the product to show through and the founder's signature on each bottle connotes a sense of craft behind each flavor's recipe.

DRY SODA CO.

DRY SODA CO.

DRY SODA CO.

DRY SODA CO.

DRY SODA CO.

DRY SODA CO.

DRY SODA CO.

HAPPYLEMON

DRINKIES   **CREAMY BABY**   **MISS PUDDING**

Project _ Happylemon Brand Visual Establishment
Design Agency _ Point-Blank Design Ltd.
Design _ Lawrence Choy, Jack Wong, Chi-Hoi Lam
Client _ Happylemon International Limited

As the management has a high expectation in the branch expansion internationally, we use an extensive and catchy way of graphic language and interior design to differentiate this brand from the traditional drink selling brand. As of end of 2011, Happylemon has expanded to more than 100 stores in Greater China and her foot print can now also be found in Australia, Singapore and Philippine.

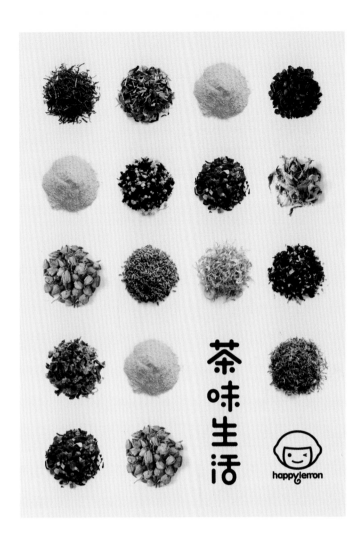

HAPPYLEMON
TEA LIFE

Project _ Happylemon Tea Life Concept
Design Agency _ Point-Blank Design Ltd.
Design _ Lawrence Choy, Kay Ching, Chi-Hoi Lam
Client _ Happylemon International Limited

An experimental brand variant developed as a new concept. The store is located in The ONE, Tsim Sha Tsui, Hong Kong, China. Introducing real tea enjoyment by offering tea leaf products and premium tea drinks.

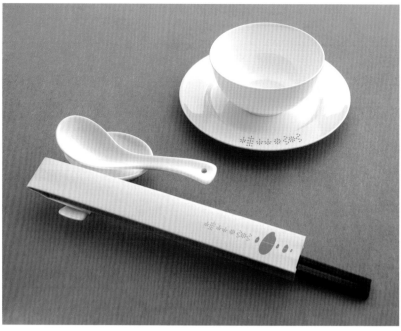

GUILIN GRUEL

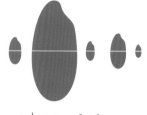

Project _ Guilin Gruel
Design Agency _ Linshaobin Design
Design _ Lin Shaobin
Client _ Guilin Gruel

Guilin Gruel is a restaurant for congee. The creative point is "rice" and the identity modeling is beautiful scenery of Guilin. The design is simple, rhythmic and full of imagination.

SLOWLY DOES IT

Project _ Slowly Does It
Design Agency _ BERG
Design _ Daniel Freytag
Client _ Slowly Does It

We needed to convey the clients passion and no-nonsense approach to food. Selecting a robust typeface and monochromatic palette gets the message across loud and clear, whilst the inclusion of the clients own quotes delivers meaning and depth to the brand.

These were then applied to environmentally responsible packaging materials. The use of craft paper stocks and the absence of embellishments helps convey the natural goodness of the product. Clean, simple and honest - "It's all about the food".

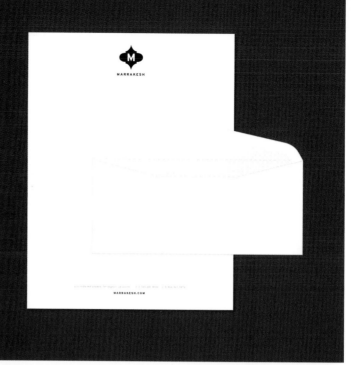

MARRAKESH

ANDREW GLEDHILL
chief marketing officer

4235 redwood avenue, los angeles, ca 90066
t: 1 310.881.8000 | f: 1 310.305.3979 | andrew@marrakesh.com
MARRAKESH.COM

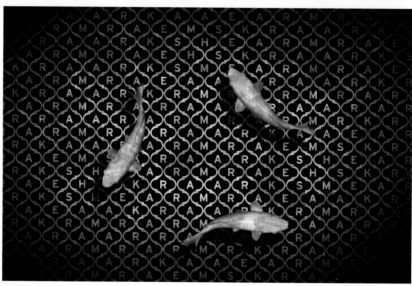

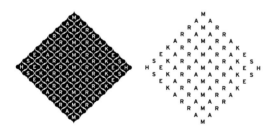

MARRAKESH

Project _ Marrakesh
Design Agency _ Groundzero Advertising
ECD _ Curt Detweiler
Art Direction _ Patrick Lin
Design _ Patrick Lin
Client _ Liquidity, Inc.

Marrakesh is a mint and tea flavored vodka from Morocco.
We designed an identity and visual language along with
packaging, interior design, and collateral to capture the
classic yet contemporary essence of Marrakesh.

Project _ Yiyang Black Tea
Design Agency _ Ruiyids
Creative Direction _ Hu Changfa
Art Direction _ Xia Dan
Design _ Hu Changfa
Copywriter _ Xia Dan

Brand identity for a famous tea in
China - Yiyang Black Tea.

A WISP OF TEA

Project _ A Wisp of Tea
Design Agency _ Linshaobin Design
Design _ Lin Shaobin
Photography _ Yan Peng
Client _ Guangdong Yawei Biotechnology Co,.Ltd

A Wisp of Tea is a tea brand under Guangdong Yawei Biotechnology Co,.Ltd. It is originated from Anxi, Fujian Province, China. The tea trees are planted in the mountains. It's a type of wild tea.

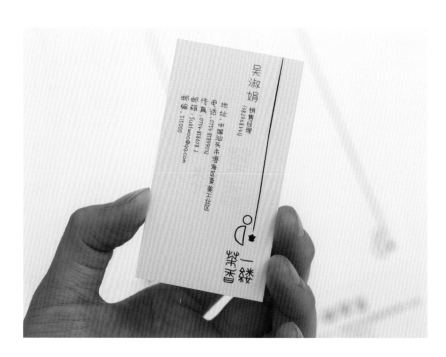

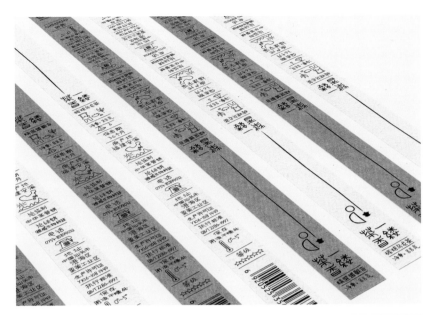

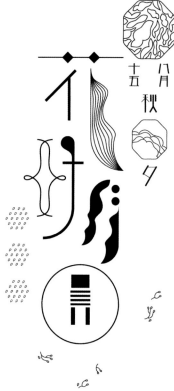

PBDL MOON FESTIVAL CELEBRATION

Project _ PBDL Moon Festival Celebration
Design Agency _ Point-Blank Design Ltd.
Design _ Lawrence Choy, Kay Ching, Jessie Lo

Moon festival is one of the major celebration among Chinese community. In addition to offering traditional mooncakes, we think that it's also a moment to share our views of creating elegant Chinese typography and clean packing design. A set of Chinese typography and symbol was created to illustrate the poetic picture of the fall season. Paper we chose has played an important role in this packing design as well.

Project _ Tai Cheong Bakery Product Brand
and Packing
Design Agency _ Point-Blank Design Ltd.
Design _ Lawrence Choy, Isabella Cheung
Client _ Tai Cheong Bakery

Redesign the image of a legendary bakery in
Hong Kong, China. Beside it's famous Chris
Patten egg tart, Tai Cheong has extended
it's product into different categories from
traditional Cantonese snacks to drinks. A
series of product identity were designed to
facilitate the client to position their product
more efficiently.

Project _ C'MON Leisure Restaurant
Design Agency _ VBN BRAND DESIGN
Design _ Venco, TAO
Client _ C'MON

"Time", "Location", "People" ... , that is the style of C'MON's design.

We do not design the brand just for "recognition", as brand design is not simply just about the "impression". In C'MON, we intend to communicate through designs to fulfill the true potential of brand designing.

C'MON

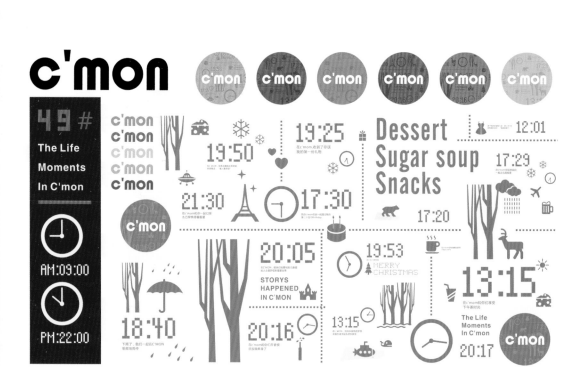

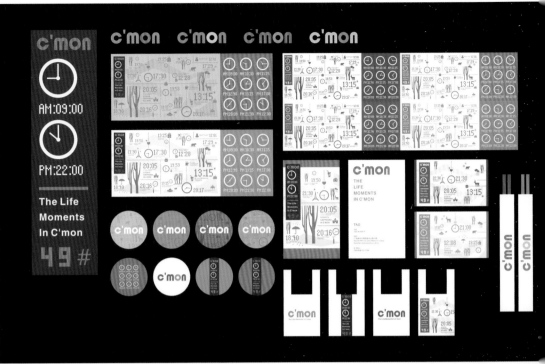

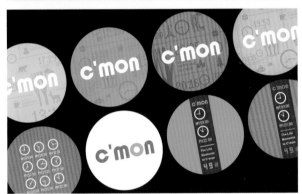

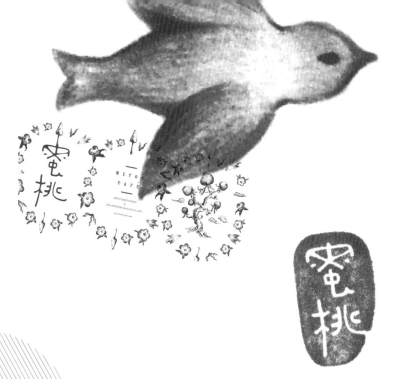

METOO CAFÉ

Project _ Metoo Café
Design Agency _ Bobchen Design Office Hangzhou
Design _ Bob Chen
Client _ Hangzhou Metoo Restaurant Management Co., Ltd.

Memories is put together by the way of game. The free-form illustration is the blue colour of celadon flower. The designer used environmentally friendly elements to express the life style of Metoo Café. The style of the project was a combination of modern and traditional features.

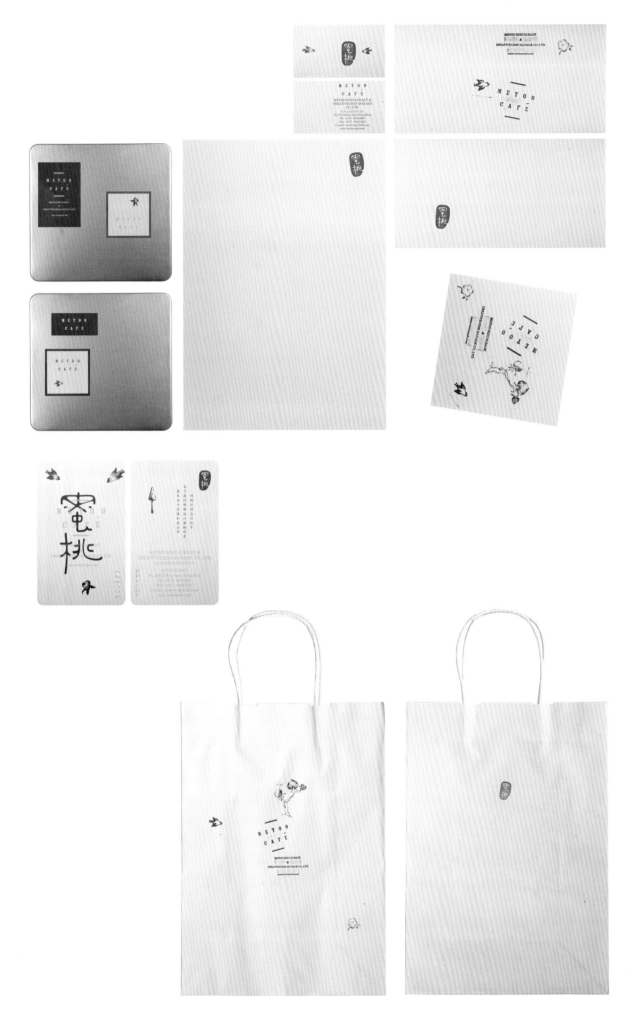

BAO BEI CHINESE BRASSERIE

Project _ Bao Bei Chinese Brasserie
Design Agency _ Glasfurd & Walker
Client _ Bao Bei Chinese Brasserie

The brief was to create a memorable and distinctive identity and brand design for the restaurant Bao Bei Chinese Brasserie in Vancouver's Chinatown. Inspired by old Shanghai, the restaurant and its identity was to feel naturally Chinese - not heavily "themed" and bring together elements of contemporary design with historical nuances that serve to infuse the brand and space with a distinctive persona and atmosphere. The identity and collateral was to feel diverse and varied with elements that the diners could discover as they interacted with each piece.

Project _ Cowboy Seven Brand Identity & Packing Design
Design Agency _ Point-Blank Design Ltd.
Design _ Lawrence Choy, Stephen Wong
Client _ Delish Brands Management Ltd.

As a cafe brand asking for a new touch and theme to the cafe market, we were asked to develop a set of packaging design to bring in new approach to redefine the Western Cowboy concept to this American drink Cafe. Having using the wild west elements, the details are retouched in a finer way to eliminate the traditional rough and wild appearance.

COWBOY SEVEN

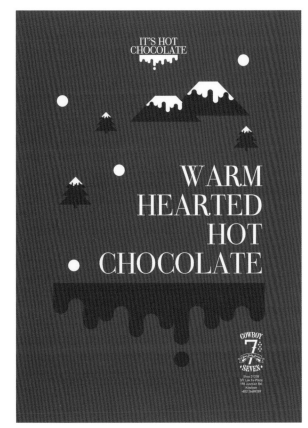

Project _ Marmalade Toast
Design Agency _ &Larry
Creative Direction _ Larry Peh
Design _ Lee Weicong
Client _ The Marmalade Group

A fresh new identity for an upmarket gourmet café from The Marmalade Group. Previously known as "Toast", the café's brandmark has been refreshed to include "Marmalade" as a headline and co-branding element.

The letters for "TOAST" are rendered vertically in a custom typeface with truncated baselines, reminiscent of bread slices popping out of a toaster. Slightly rounded-off corners at the bottom of the letters are reminiscent of melted cheese on toast.

All in all, a simple and evocative design that is elegant, informal and full of visual flavour as applied across store signage, cups, bags, menu, wrappers and food tags.

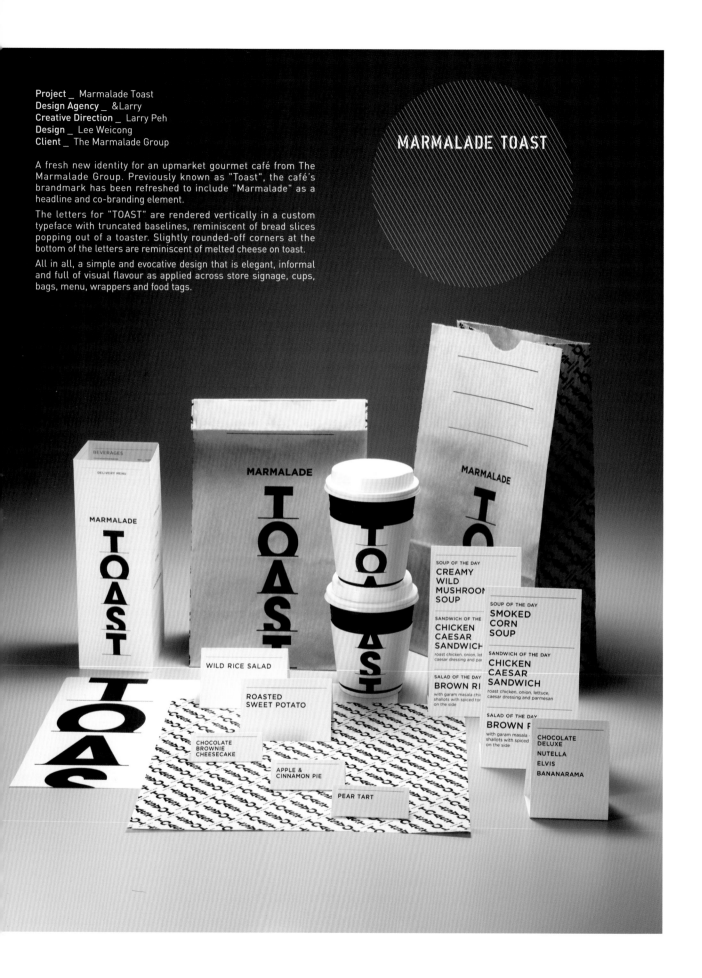

MARMALADE

TOAST

Project _ Line One Restaurant
Design Agency _ VBN BRAND DESIGN
Design _ Venco, TAO
Client _ Mr. Ray

From market environment to customer responses, Line-one carries out a full-scale innovative reformation. As a result, a more harmonic relationship with the city and the customers is created.

Through the design with "double-yellow line" connecting the shop and the main road along with various interesting traffic signs and unique carriage design, we achieve the uniqueness as well as the practical utility. With the geometrically crafted zebra crossing, a peculiar visual effect is brought to the customers alive. These details reflects the Line-one's spirit of "entertaining through innovation".

LINE ONE
RESTAURANT

Project _ RBT Tea Cafe Brand Upgrade Establishment
Design Agency _ Point-Blank Design Ltd.
Design _ Lawrence Choy, Isabella Cheung
Client _ RBT International Limited

Evolving from original RBT, Shanghai market demands
a newer RBT image. The new image applies from brand
logo, visual system and restaurant interior design.

RBT

LET'S HAVE
SOME TEA &
CONTINUE TO TALK
ABOUT
HAPPY THINGS

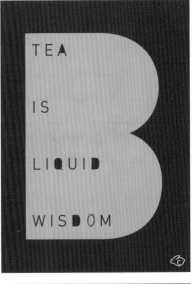

TEA
IS
LIQUID
WISDOM

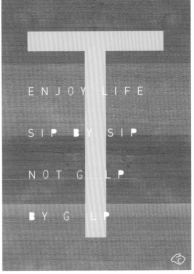

ENJOY LIFE
SIP BY SIP
NOT GULP
BY GULP

LOVE
IS THE
BEST
SWEETENER
OF TEA

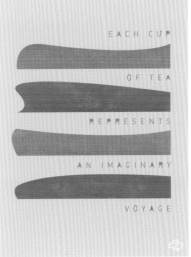

EACH CUP
OF TEA
REPRESENTS
AN IMAGINARY
VOYAGE

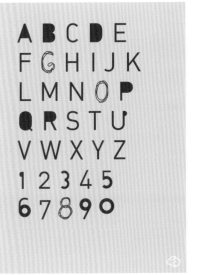

A B C D E
F G H I J K
L M N O P
Q R S T U
V W X Y Z
1 2 3 4 5
6 7 8 9 0

HONEY CAKE

Project _ HONEY Cake
Design Agency _ Linshaobin Design
Design _ Lin Shaobin, Ma Xiaoqing
Client _ HONEY Cake

HONEY Cake is a Western-style bakery chain store. The unique feature is to use honey, instead of sugar. All the cakes are delicious with a sweet honey flavor.

We used the color characteristics of honeycomb and bee to create the logo design in the form of a HONEY font. The whole identity is like a piece of HONEY cake.

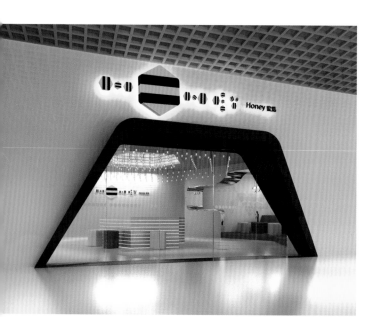

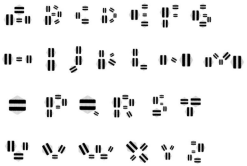

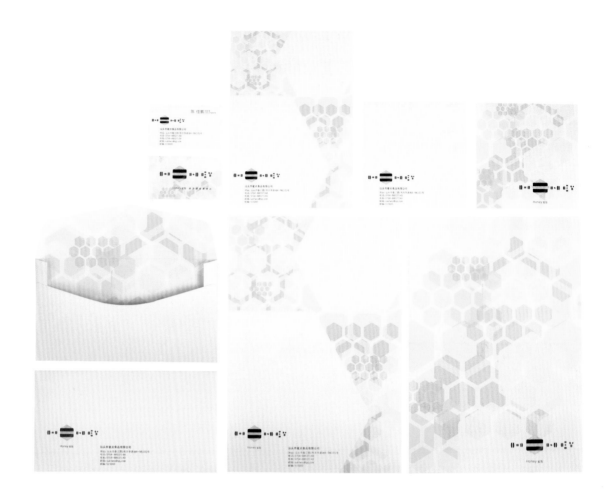

JOYFUL DESSERT

Project _ Joyful Dessert
Design Agency _ VBN BRAND DESIGN
Design _ Venco, TAO, Zero
Client _ Joyful Dessert

"Joyful Dessert" is a Dessert Branch specialized in Hong Kong-style Dessert making. We seek to create home atmosphere to welcome our guests. Through unique local style, we make our guests recall the memory of the traditional culture of Hong Kong, China blending its historical and modern elements into one.

In "Joyful Dessert", people from different backgrounds enjoy together, share and create happiness and laughter. Undoubtedly, "Joyful Dessert" is a place full of smile and welcome!

Project _ CHINA POBLANO NOODLES & TACOS
Design Agency _ Toormix
Design _ Oriol Armengou, Ferran Mitjans
Interior Design _ Seed Design
Product photography _ Thomas Schauer
Interior photography _ Jeff Green
Client _ Think Food Group - chef José Andrés

China Poblano is a Mexican and Chinese restaurant located in Cosmopolitan Hotel Las Vegas and directed by chef José Andrés. The identity design plays with the iconography of both cultures and we've developed different graphics for the restaurant: menus, cards, napkins, stickers, ... and some elements of the facade and interior of the restaurant.

**CHINA POBLANO
NOODLES & TACOS**

**CHI
NA
PO
BLA
NO**
BY
JOSÉ ANDRÉS

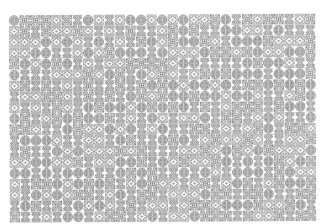

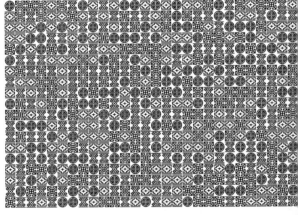

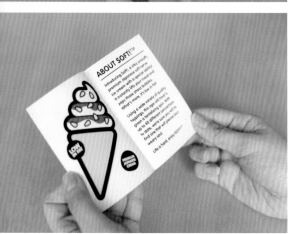

SOFT! SOFTSERVE ICECREAM

Project _ SOFT! Softserve Icecream
Design Agency _ Bravo Company
Creative Direction _ Edwin Tan
Illustration _ Amanda Ho
Client _ SOFT!

Soft!, a silky smooth soft-serve ice cream using premium Japanese cream that's great with zapping those stress bubbles. In synch with the brand's marketing campaign as the ice-cream that zaps, the press kit is in the form of a Happiness Kit. It is equipped with a Happiness Guidebook that dedicates ice cream flavors as remedies for modern day stress. Think computer crashes and losing the winning lottery ticket.

The retail space was designed to be a shop within a shop to give customers an interesting experience while dining in or taking out. Okay we are lying. We brought the shop front into the shop itself because we weren't allowed to make changes to the aesthetically-challenging facade.

IGLOO ZOO

Project _ Igloo Zoo
Creative Direction _ Fabio Ongarato
Design _ Byron George, Andrea Wilcock
Client _ Igloo Zoo

Igloo Zoo is Australia's first super-chilled yoghurt bar. Fabio Ongarato Design were commissioned to create a complete brand experience from the identity and packaging right through to the interior design.

Taking the inspiration from an igloo shape and the product itself we created a branded environment that reflects the notion of an igloo's inner sanctum. The outside is clad in shinny black circular tiles which heightens and juxtaposes with the pure white interior. The interior is made from sensual, curvilinear lines with glossy white epoxy floor. A limed timber screen meanders around the store, providing enclosure and warmth while referencing both the "zoo" and "igloo". Graphics are subtly used as wallpaper in the space – a large circle was created to the exterior to house the main sign which is made of white neon.

Project _ The Marmalade Pantry Corporate Identity
Design Agency _ &Larry
Creative Direction _ Larry Peh
Design Agency _ Lee Weicong
Client _ The Marmalade Group

We created an organic and minimalist identity for this popular and upmarket café that prides itself on offering "good things to eat". The custom logotype sits in a silhouette that resembles fresh bread, cupcakes, fruits, cheeses, vegetables and meats. A series of advertisements was created for the launch of the new flagship café, featuring simple photographs of key ingredients for signature dishes on the menu. The purity and goodness of the foods come across directly to whet readers' appetites. The brandmark is always stamped front and centre to claim ownership of this branding trait.

Project _ Gabbani Identity
Design Agency _ DEMIAN CONRAD DESIGN
Design _ Demain Conrad
Photography _ Olivier Lovey, Sylvain Meltz
Client _ Gabbani

Gabbani is the oldest delicatessen in the Swiss Italian part (1937). It is an old family business that survived and flourished until becoming the state-of-the-art reference in the food industry. 30 people are working to serve the best as possible to their customers. The company is divided in the following sectors: food (vegetables and fruits, meet, wine and spirits, flowers, bread and pasta, G product line), restaurant, bed&breakfast and catering.

For Gabbani we have created the new identity and few promotional campaigns. The idea behind the project was to create a fashionable and bold identity in order to stand out from the crowd in a competitive market. Visually the references are from the flavour of the 30's with a mix of various typographies and the use of the black&white optical art typical of the 60's.

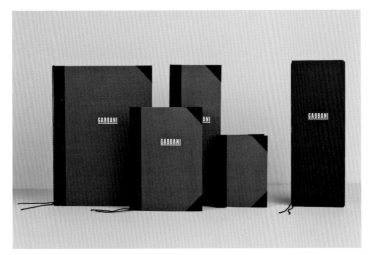

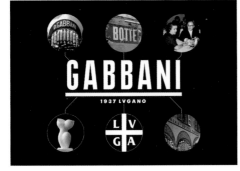

moomah   moomah   moomah

Project _ Moomah
Design Agency _ Apartment One
Client _ Moomah

When we first met with the client, Tracey Stewart, she expressed a desire for Moomah to be a space that encourages creativity and connection between parents, caregivers, children and friends. A place where imagination is king, where we are inspired by our children and hope to be able to inspire them, and teach them that anything is possible. We created three different variations of the M logo out of elements that visually represented each of the four core brand values: connect, create, discover, and nourish. Moomah being a space created to encourage parents, children and friends to connect, create discover, and nourish their relationships to one another, themselves, and the world around them.

We also wanted to create a memorable and recognizable brand language without putting a logo on all applications. We created custom, application-specific illustrations filled with the wonder, magic, and heart of Moomah and placed them above a dotted line and type to set the foundation for our brand language. These illustrations and corresponding tag lines were conceptually developed for their specific applications.

MOOMAH

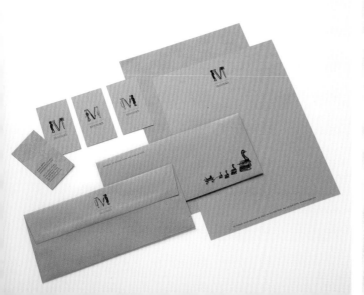

Project _ Möoi
Design Agency _ SeventhDesign™
Design _ Bruno Siriani
Client _ Grupo Multifood

Möoi is part of a brand new concept in Buenos Aires: the contemporaneous food. This wave has been merged in this project with the modern art & design to build a nice space, comfortable and very impressive utilizing a great amount of different shapes, textures and colors. SeventhDesign™ developed a huge number of graphic pieces such as business cards, various letterheads, stickers, packaging, food and wine menus, etc. and a lot more industrial pieces for the interior and the exterior of the space.

The brand elements, graphic design, packaging and industrial design provides a strong image to this beautiful restaurant located into Belgrano town, Buenos Aires.

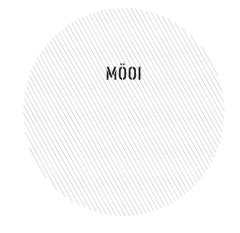

LO FONDA DEL SOL

Project _ La Fonda del Sol
Design Agency _ Mirko Ilic Corp.
Creative Direction _ Mirko Ilic
Art Direction _ Mirko Ilic
Design _ Jee-eun Lee, Mirko Ilic
Client _ Patina Restaurant Group

Identity, signage, and collateral design for La Fonda del Sol restaurant in New York.

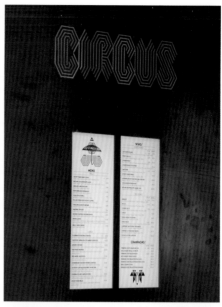

CIRCUS

Project _ Circus Identity
Design Agency _ Mind Design
Creative Direction _ Holger Jacobs
Art Direction _ Craig Sinnamon
Design _ Andy Lang, Sara Streule
Interior design _ Tom Dixon / Design Research Studio
Client _ Circus

Identity for a new club and restaurant with a burlesque theme and changing performances. Since the club interior features many mirrored surfaces, the design of the logo is based on the shape of a kaleidoscope. The outline shape and basic construction of the logo always remains the same while the inside changes depending on its application. Other influences came from Surrealism, Art Deco, Alice in Wonderland, animals and the steps leading up to the large table that doubles as a stage. A main feature of the interior is a 3-dimensional version of the logo built from different layers of perspex, set into a wall and illuminated from the back in changing colours. Collaboration with Design Research Studio.

Project _ Plus & Minus Magazine Conception Restaurant
Design Agency _ VBN BRAND DESIGN
Creative Direction _ VENCO
Art Direction _ VENCO
Design _ VENCO, Qangzz, LEA, TAO, BONE
Client _ Plus & Minus Restaurant Chains

High Quality, Good Taste - the motto we put forward for the modern fast dining was unforgettable experience. Plus & Minus advocates the concept that the body and the spirit should be dining together and introduce the magazines and information into the dining room. At the same time, customers can have a unique taste and unforgettable experience here.

PLUS & MINUS
MAGAZINE
CONCEPTION
RESTAURANT

Project _ Spudbar
Design Agency _ Truly Deeply
Brand Strategy _ Peter Singline
Creative Direction _ David Ansett
Design Direction _ Cassandra Gill
Design _ Lachlan McDougall & Cassandra Gill
Typography _ Lachlan McDougall & Cassandra Gil
Illustration _ Veronica Fever
Writers _ Dave Ansett & Peter Singline
Finish Artist _ Rachel O'Brien
Client _ Spudbar

Spudbar was founded in Melbourne in 2000, born out of a frustration at the lack of a healthy, great tasting feed that was quick, convenient and value for money. When we began working with Spudbar they had 9 stores around Australia and were struggling to own a space in the market compelling enough to grow the business to the next level.

We immersed ourselves in their market segment, generated some clear qualitative market insights, and led a brand strategy re-think to provide a clear vision for where the brand and its offer could most potently be positioned for success in the market. The key to developing the Spudbar brand identity and retail environment to match the newly defined brand proposition was all about unlocking the visual cues of the classic, one-off local cafe. By unlocking the code of visual language for these unique, high-loyalty, non-franchise food businesses, we developed the Spudbar brand identity to work in a similar, non-cookie cutter manner.

SPUDBAR

Project _ Meat & Bread
Design Agency _ Glasfurd & Walker
Client _ Meat & Bread

Identity and brand design for Gastown's latest addition to the neighbourhood, Meat & Bread.

The studio was approached to created a strong, masculine identity and brand design which communicates the restaurant's simple and uncomplicated offer. With a focus on a daily roasted meat, a visual system was needed to communicate what was on offer each day. For this, a series of icons was created which complimented the core logo and extended the identity onto packaging for products and take out. The design had to be clean and minimal with a timeless aspect to the identity without feeling "retro". Strength through simplicity was the ultimate mandate.

MEAT & BREAD

FASHION

Project _ 11th Moon
Design Agency _ RoAndCo
Creative Direction _ Roanne Adams
Design _ Tadeu Magalhães, Cynthia Ratsabouth
Client _ 11th Moon

11th Moon is a clothing boutique in Laguna Beach, CA. Inspired by owner, Virginia's love of astronomy, we created a graphic system representative of scientific constellations, phases of the moon, and a selection of celestial symbols. The new branding set 11th Moon apart from competitors in the area and quickly led the store to build up a following, carrying independent designer lines like – Timo Weiland, Arnsdorf, VPL, etc.

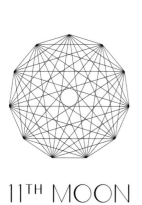

MÚM
M MÚM

Project _ MÚM
Design Agency _ TYMOTE
Client _ MÚM

Developed a branding for a fashion
brand called "MÚM". Provided art
direction and artwork.

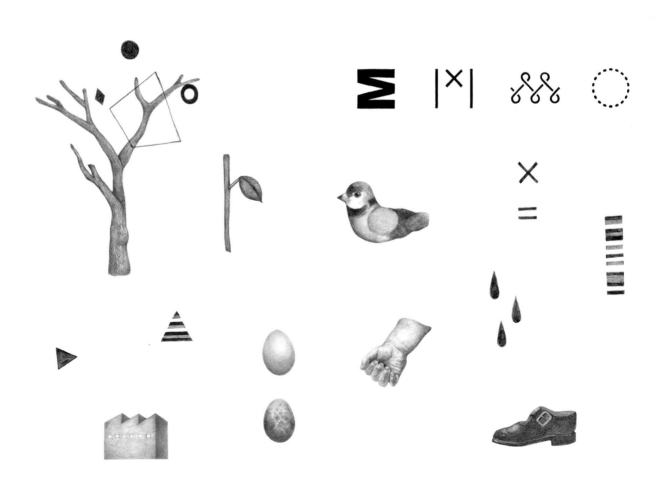

Project _ Flyer; SPIKE
Design Agency _ Fujimoto Gumi
Design _ Kohichi Fujimoto
Client _ Flyer; SPIKE

Flier of select shop and production of tag and paper bag.

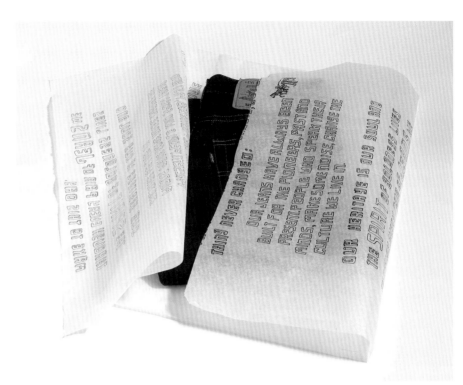

Project _ Levi's Packaging
Design Agency _ Checkland Kindleysides
Client _ Levi Strauss

New packaging launched with new store concept.

LEVI'S

Project _ Converse
Concept & Design _ ...,staat creative agency
Photography _ Converse, ...,staat creative agency
Client _ Converse Inc.

"Famous icons connected by Chucks" was the brand campaign developed by Anomaly in New York. Converse Inc. approached ...,staat creative agency to develop a design direction and retail concept for Europe, as well as directing the rollout and localization of the campaign. The design direction utilized the existing identity and visual language, and ...,staat introduced raw, organic and fluid elements in order to balance the clean and consistent imagery. ...,staat used personal handwriting, opaque paint and semi-transparent ink in striking black and white. These elements were taken to the next level for the retail concept: painted quotes, black-dipped objects and high-gloss white displays brought the Converse icons to life. For the localization of the campaign, ...,staat collaborated with European artists from the past, present and future, such as Ian Curtis, Herman Brood, Asia Argento, Carlos Diez Diez, Vive la Fete and Jeferson Hack to acknowledge the long Converse history and continuing style endurance.

CONVERSE

ELTTOBTEP
ISSEY MIYAKE

Project _ ELTTOB TEP ISSEY MIYAKE
Design Agency _ Artless Inc.
Art Direction _ shun kawakami
Design _ shun kawakami
Client _ ISSEY MIYAKE INC.

Gift packagings for Online store (http : //store. elttobtep. com/) of ELTTOB TEP ISSEY MIYAKE.

Project _ Lacoste Eco – Techno Polo by Tom Dixon
Design Agency _ Mind Design
Concept _ Tom Dixon
Creative Director _ Holger Jacobs
Client _ Tom Dixon

Collaboration with Tom Dixon. Packaging and launch graphics for two special edition polo shirts commissioned by Lacoste. Tom's concept was to explore two very different materials and the technology used in the production process of the garment. The most eco-friendly way to package the eco polo was not to print on the packaging at all but use embossing instead. The techno polo is vacuum-packaged in screen-printed foil.

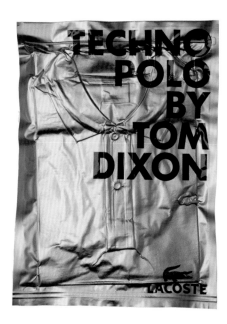
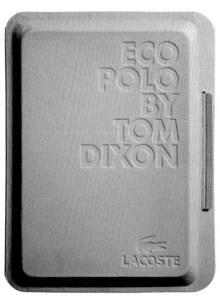

déjanos   jugar   Calle

CALLE FAVELA SHOE

Project _ Calle Favela Shoe
Design Agency _ Hort
Creative direction _ David Young (Calle)
Art direction _ Hort
Design _ Hort
Client _ Calle

Calle commissioned us to brand their new shoe named Favela. We designed the type treatment, the sole of the shoe, the shoebox and some promotional material like posters.

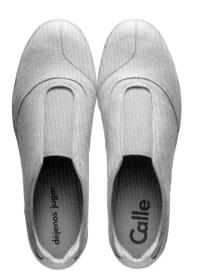

Project _ Adidas Originals Green Collection
Design Agency _ Studio Intraligi
Design _ Philippe Intraligi
Apparel Design _ Camilla Veth
Marketing _ Erika Benz
Client _ Adidas Originals

The collection consists of sustainable shoes and apparel made of eco-friendly materials such as cork, recycled gum, hemp, jute, recycled EVA, wood, grass and recycled garments. I designed several pattern, icons and apparel graphics around this theme of collaged, mixed materials, wrapping it into the spirit of sportive, fashionable clothing.

ADIDAS ORIGINALS

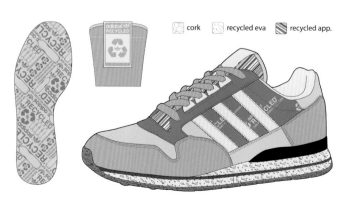

cork   recycled eva   recycled app.

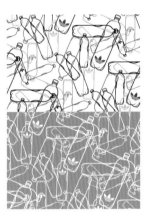

MICHAEL SONTAG

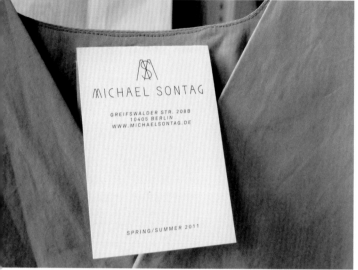

Project _ Michael Sontag
Design Agency _ Eps51 Graphic Design Studio
Design _ Ben Wittner, Sascha Thoma
Lookbook Photography _ Christian Schwarzenberg
Client _ Michael Sontag

Michael Sontag is Berlin's latest fashion talent. Exploring original cuts and combining finest natural materials with new-age active fabrics he creates clean and elegant looks for a sophisticated market.

We developed a very individual, elegant logotype and signet which can be combined differently on diverse types of media.

Michael Sontag's corporate identity is very light while leaving a strong mark on the viewer.

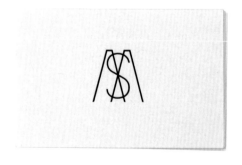

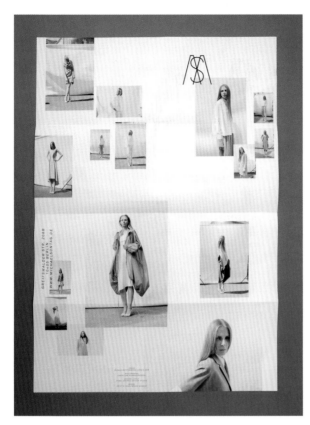

FUN FUN WONG

Project _ Missman Conceptual Fashion Collection
Creative Direction _ Fun Fun Wong, Kila Cheung
Art Direction _ Fun Fun Wong
Fashion Design _ Fun Fun Wong
Graphic Design _ Kila Cheung
On Show _ Hong Kong Convention and Exhibition Center, Grand Hall

Our concept of doing a collection is to carry some message to communicate and to share with others.

miss man is a collection that sharing about new style of women: they have strong characteristic but still trapped by the lock of traditional Chinese culture. now, woman's new style is still in progress to establish, miss man is reflecting this contradiction and instable status.

143

Project _ Pladis & María Vogel
Design Agency _ Anagrama
Client _ Pladis & María Vogel

María Vogel is Latin America's up and coming fashion designer. Our goal for this project was to develop a brand that was convincing, sober, and above all, portrayed Maria's vision, all this without competing with her imposing designs.

Project _ Gap Body Fit Brand Identity
Design Agency _ Manual
Creative Direction _ Tom Crabtree
Art Direction _ Tom Crabtree
Design _ Tom Crabtree, Eileen Lee, Gary Williams
Copywriter _ David Begler
Photography _ Vanessa Chu
Client _ Gap Inc.

Brand identity, print and packaging for Gap Body Fit, a new range of women's athletic.

Apparel from Gap. The abstract "G" symbol hints at a bended figure – communicating the idea of flexibility and agility.

GAP BODY FIT

GapBodyFit

Project _ Brand Identity Design, Fashion Show Collateral
Design Agency _ RoAndCo
Creative Direction _ Roanne Adams
Design _ Tadeu Magalhães, Cynthia Ratsabouth
Client _ Timo Weiland

Timo Weiland, an up-and-coming designer, wanted to take his brand from a relatively unknown line to an established Men's and Women's ready-to-wear collection. Inspired by Timo's love of classic tailoring, unisex accessories and modern elegance, we combined ideas of refined classicism, quirky details and contemporary street-style to create a uniquely "Timo" identity. We art directed and designed the collateral for Timo's debut Spring'10 and subsequent Fall'10 presentations.

PIAFF BOUTIQUE

Project _ Branding for PIAFF
Design Agency _ Marc Kandalaft Design
Design _ Marc Kandalaft
Client _ PIAFF Boutique

PIAFF branding and packaging, Business cards,
promotional tools (post cards / photography),
bags and rubans, posters, window / vitrine
concepts and more.

ALPHA
MENS—WEAR
(SHOREDITCH)

LONDON
&
東京

ALPHALONDONDOTCOM

SELF/EDGE JAPANESE DENIM
by
EDWIN JEANS, LEE VINTAGE JEANS, BLUEBELL JEANS by
WRANGLER, STUDIO D'ARTISAN, ALLEVOL, TROUSERS
LONDON JEANS, DENHAM JEANS & CARHARTT JEANS.

Project _ ALPHA
Design Agency _ BERG
Design _ Daniel Freytag
Client _ Alpha

The "Alpha" male concept runs through all
branded communication. By using imagery
of the North Alaskan timber wolf we evoke a
sense of danger and raw power. This combined
with a strong colour palette of reds and black
with minimalist typographic treatments results
in a confident, sophisticated and provocative
brand identity.

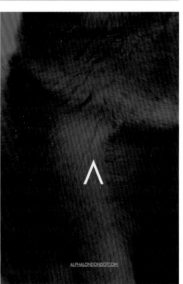

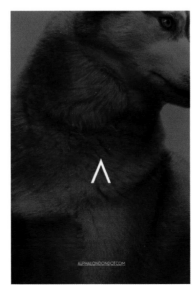

BAO BAO

ISSEY MIYAKE

Project _ BAO BAO ISSEY MIYAKE
Design Agency _ Taku Satoh Design Office Inc.
Art Direction _ Taku Satoh
Design _ Taku Satoh, Shingo Noma
Photography _ Yasuaki Yoshinaga
Client _ ISSEY MIYAKE INC.

This is an ad poster for BAO BAO ISSEY MIYAKE. We have taken the structure of the bag based on a basic triangular pattern and applied it into the production process of the BAO BAO logo. Additionally, we have incorporated the numerous unique logos that were created in the process of the logo production into the ad visual. The significance of this poster is that an infinite number of different bags can be created from this single basic pattern. The method of defining a rule to create an infinite number of ideas is the same as the Haiku rule of 5-7-5 that has enabled the composition of an eternal number of poems.

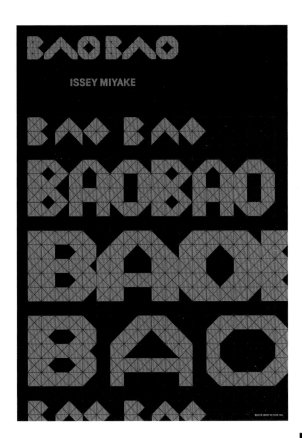

ISSEY MIYAKE

ISSEY MIYAKE

ELTTOB TEP
ISSEY MIYAKE / GINZA

Project _ ELTTOB TEP ISSEY MIYAKE / GINZA
Design Agency _ Taku Satoh Design Office Inc.
Art Director _ Taku Satoh
Direction _ Taku Satoh , Shingo Noma
Photography _ Yasuaki Yoshinaga
Client _ ISSEY MIYAKE INC.

Among ISSEY MIYAKE INC.'s numerous brands, ELTTOB TEP ISSEY MIYAKE is a new business category store where only selected garments are showcased. ELTTOB TEP ISSEY MIYAKE / SEMBA opened in the spring of 2007 in Osaka, this was followed by the opening of its second store ELTTOB TEP ISSEY MIYAKE / GINZA in Ginza, Tokyo in spring of 2011. We oversee everything related to designs ranging from the naming to logo, graphics, store, furniture, window display and ads. The naming concept for ELTTOB TEP can be understood if you read it backwards. In Japan, the container used to bottle mineral water is known as PET BOTTLE. In other words, we simply reversed the name of the most common everyday object. It represents the store's concept of taking the concept of a common object and reversing it.

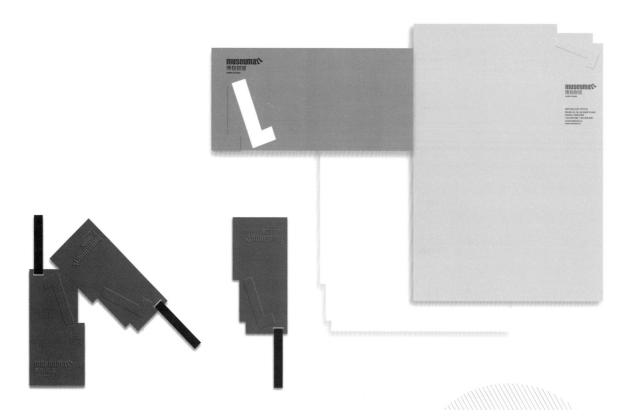

Project _ Museumall
Design Agency _ 5W.1H Brand Solution Ltd
Design _ Heng Aik-soon, Wilson
Credits _ Heng Aik-soon Wilson, Kai Hu, Lw Jie, Gary Choi and 5W.1H teams
Client _ Museumall Limited

Museumall is a collection of variety ranges of shoe and also a "shopping museum" of a national chain brand for taste, fashion, lifestyle and value.

For the naming of the brand, we added "mall" in English and "Wu (物)" in Chinese, which directly echoes the characteristics of diverse products and infiltrates personality and humor. It adds a little bit of fun for the mature men in life.

From dinosaur bones, bone shoes to stationery, promotion materials, advertising and other promotion, the core is the brand philosophy of Museumall to form a well-built brand image as a whole with a deep impression.

MUSEUMALL

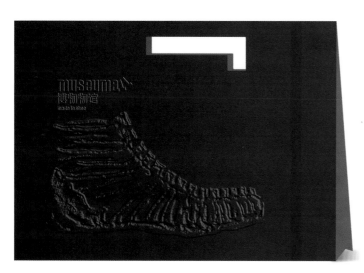

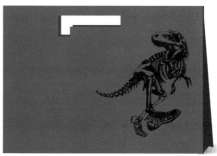

museuma⼈
博物物馆
made in shoe

museuma⼈
博物物馆
made in shoe

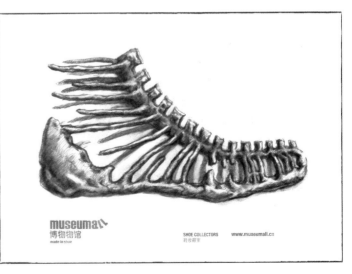

LALUNA

Project _ LaLuna Boutique Branding
Design Agency _ THERE Design
Design _ Paul Taboure, Jon Zhu
Client _ LaLuna

LaLuna is a high-end women's fashion boutique. We worked closely with award-winning interior designer Matt Sheargold to create a refined, yet eclectic retail experience. Everything from identity, labeling, stationery, receipt wallets, carry bags and in-store display items through to invites, signage, and a retail website were produced for their successful launch.

Project _ Aishti Identity
Design Agency _ Sagmeister inc.
Art Direction _ Stefan Sagmeister
Design & Illustration _ Jessica Walsh, Jong Woo Si, Joe Shouldice, Jonathan Puckey
Photography _ Henry Hargreaves
Client _ Aishti

Identity and packaging design for Aishti, Aizone, and Minis department stores. For Aishti's new identity, we honed in on the dots above the "i" in the logo and created a series of graphic patterns which were used across Aishti's stationary, wrapping & tissue paper, gift cards, garment bags, credit cards, stickers, and more. The Aishti gift bags each feature a surprise inside: kissing couples. Aizone bags featured optical illusions inside the bags. For the minis brand we created a series of characters which were interactive with the shopping bag handles.

AÏSHTI

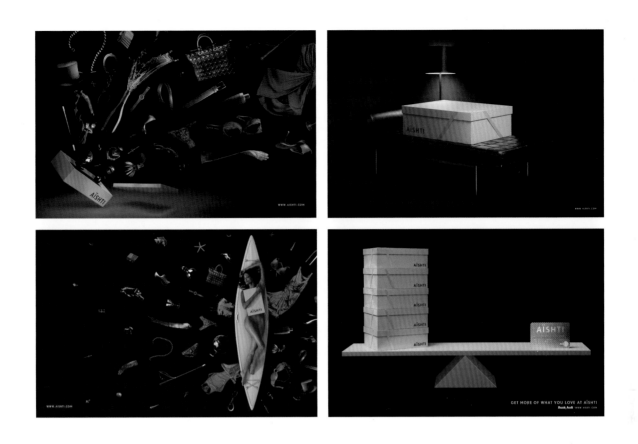

Project _ Nike Sportswear
Design Agency _ NIKE Brand Design China
Design _ James Qu
Client _ Nike

The shoe will be available with two packages: in a standard shoebox or a collectable shoebox limited to 200 pairs only. The collectable shoebox is designed to complement the shoe with the same inspiration: white box with tiger stripe prints and Chinese character " 寅 " (tiger) on Chinese trigrams and " 平安 " (peace) are embossed on each side of the shoebox. Finally, the five finger death grip design is used to open the shoebox in true tiger fashion.

NIKE SPORTSWEAR

Project _ Nike New York City Marathon 2009
Design Agency _ 2x4
Photography _ Luke Stettner
Client _ Nike

"In this city, every day's a marathon. Living in New York is daily endurance test, a real time obstacle course, a sensorial avalanche. There is a beautiful brutality to a city where everything is in flux, in process, under construction; where nothing is straight or finished or fully functional. New York is our beast: its ugly and dangerous but show it some affection and its a loyal friend forever. We're proud because we're tough. We can take it. We can absorb punishing heat and spiraling rent and bitter wind and appalling smells and it only makes us love it all the more. "Fire is the test of gold," the old saying goes, "adversity the test of strong men." Its not that we're arrogant, its just that we feel we are tested every day and every day we prove we've got the metal. 26.2? That's nothing. I commute from Queens."

2x4 produced Nike's branding for the 2009 New York City Marathon. The campaign included broadcast, posters, store windows, point of purchase displays and general morale boosts along the road.

NIKE NEW YORK
CITY MARATHON
2009

26 NYC
.2 ——— ——

Project _ Mads Nørgaard Copenhagen - Speak Up!
Design Agency _ e-Types
Design _ Jess Andersen
Photography _ Frederik Lindstrom & Hasse Nielsen
Client _ Mads Nørgaard Copenhagen

For the past five years, e-Types has been working for international fashion brand Mads Nørgaard Copenhagen, creating and advising on brand strategy and visual identity. The main initial task was moving Mads Nørgaard beyond fashion and towards culture - creating a strong and unique brand steeped in Nørgaard's cultural heritage.

Mads Nørgaard is an excellent example of how you can work strategically with a brand while breaking new ground for the fashion company and its communication. In a close collaboration with Mads Nørgaard, e-Types has developed a new brand strategy, a new visual identity, fashion shows, image campaigns, records, packaging, and fashion films.

By using elements from the world of culture referenced by Mads Nørgaard in his work and inspiration, we created a more meaningful brand. A brand that transgresses ideas of high and low culture by plucking from both worlds - just like Mads Nørgaard does in his collections. The fashion company positions itself differently from its main competitors through a genuine link to its customers' cultural context, updating its relevancy to attract a new target group while linking between the past and the present.

NIKE BASKETBALL

Project _ NIKE Basketball - The World Is Watching
Design Agency _ Hort
Art Direction (Nike) _ Michael Spoljaric
Client _ Nike

Street basketball in New York City - We worked on a Nike event named "The world is watching".

We designed the type treatment, a font, several shoeboxes (for each part of NYC) and a huge mural as an announcement for "The world is watching" street basketball event.

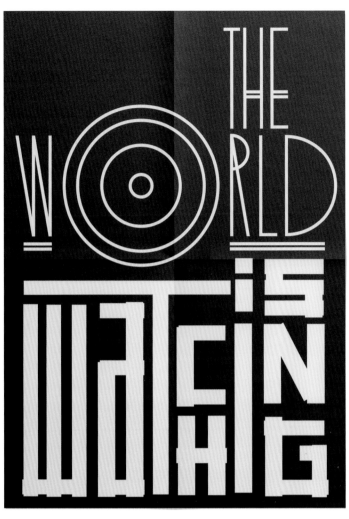

THE WORLD IS WATCHING

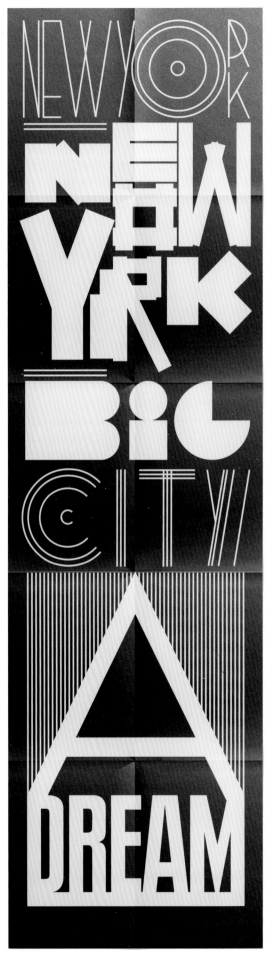

NEW YORK NEW YORK BIG CITY A DREAM

ABCDEFGHIJKLMNOP
QRSTUVWXYZ!$?.,:
1234567890 HORT

Project _ Wooonderland Corporate Identity
Design Agency _ &Larry
Creative Direction _ Larry Peh
Design _ Ter Yeow Yeong
Client _ Wooonderland

Wooonderland is an experimental fashion retail playground appealing to the young and the bold. Wooonderland shares a link to its sister store named "Actually...", with three prominent circles in place of an ellipsis. The brandmark is big, bold, and the colour palette colourful and bright, reflecting the personality of the boutique as well as the merchandise it carries. The store cards can function as fun clips for tagging magazine pages, school notes or folders. A larger metallic version is used as a swing tag to highlight and to add a touch of luxe to selected products in the store.

Project _ Pillart
Design Agency _ LonBrand
Creative Direction _ Alon
Design _ Alon, Shi Yan, Zhang He
Photography _ Tom Hines
Client _ Pillart

Pillart is the second fashion brand by LonBrand. The design is displayed by the form of capsules, which include all the evil things and negative emotions inside.

PILLART

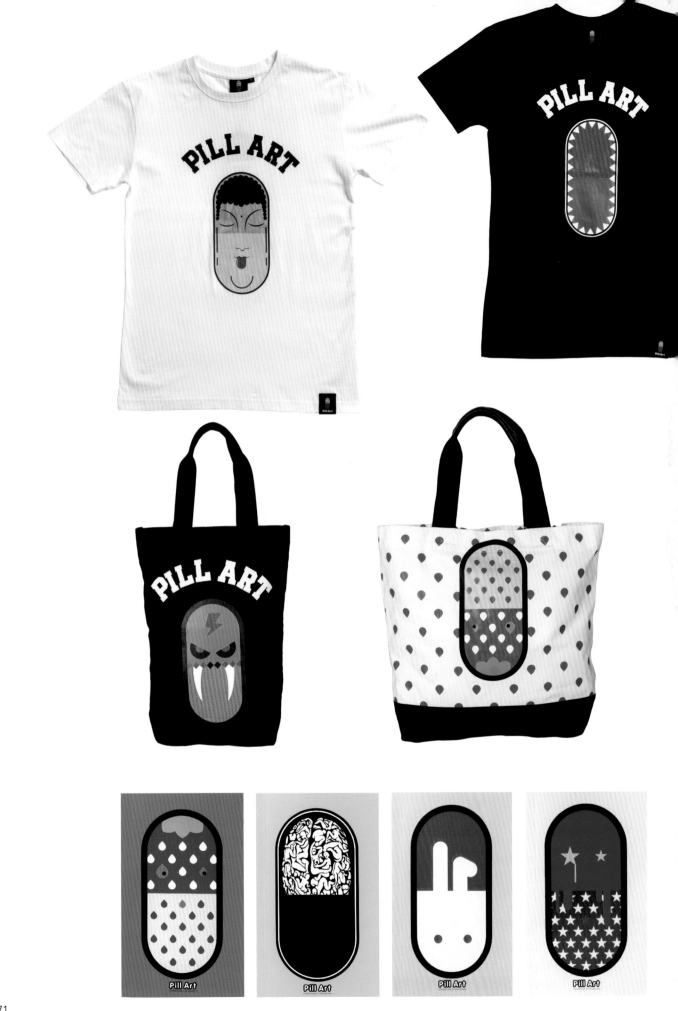

Project _ Disc Blaze 90
Design Agency _ C100 Purple Haz
Design _ Christian Hundertmark, Clemens Baldermann
Client _ PUMA

Conception, art direction and illustration for the Puma "Disc Blaze 90" launch. The full communication for the heritage shoe series includes bespoke type, window vinyl design for miscellaneous window sizes, POS / POP display and giveaway design for sneaker lifestyle shops in Germany and United Kingdom, like "Solebox" Berlin or "Size?" London.

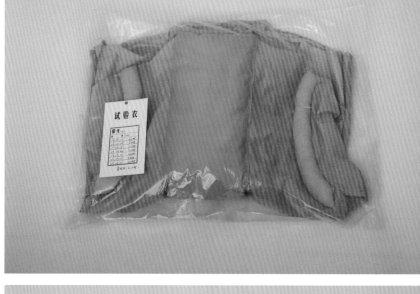

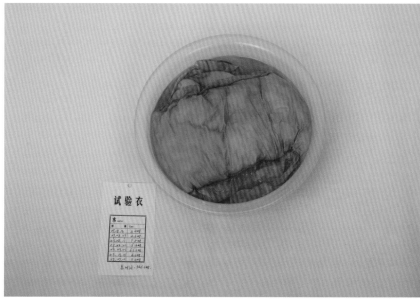

Project _ Nature View
Design _ Yao Ye, Li Xibin
Client _ Nature View

Nature has her point of view towards beauty and goodness. This is the concept of the fashion label of "Experimental Dressing". It's not finished until the dresses are bathed by sun and washed by water, after they are produced by the factory. It's perfect by the force of nature.

NATURE VIEW

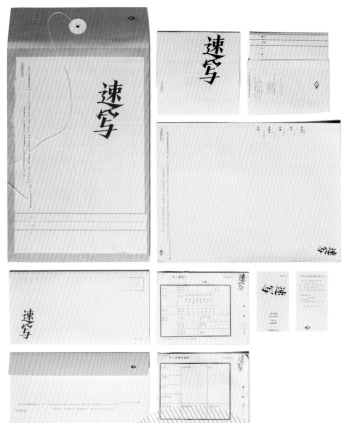

Project _ Croquis
Design Agency _ Bobchen Design Office Hangzhou
Design _ Bob Chen
Client _ JNBY

As a fashion brand since 1994, JNBY launched CROQUIS, a new high-end men's wear brand. It quickly attracts the educated young men with the spiritual awakening consciousness, thanks to its distinctive design style and value concept. The young people go after the humanistic spirit and unique way of life, which can be found in CROQUIS with a high degree of resonance.

CROQUIS

严谨 奢华
幽默 经典
诡异 工装
诗意 生活

速写

Project _ BSQT
Design Agency _ Linshaobin Design
Design _ Lin Shaobin, Peng Feng, Ma Xiaoqin
Client _ ITALY BSQT Industry Co., ltd

BSQT is a shoe brand. In order to improve BSQT brand identity, we followed the core value of the brand and redesign the new image.

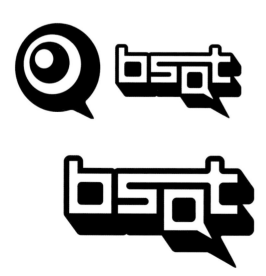

SAKS
"THINK ABOUT..."

Project _ Saks "Think About..." Campaign
Design Agency _ Pentagram Design
Design _ Michael Bierut
Client _ Saks Fifth Avenue

For the 2010 spring campaign Saks Fifth Avenue introduced a new tagline, "Think about...," a playful suggestion that shoppers consider new ways to play with their personal style via various items found at Saks. The tagline was finished with amusing statements about fashion and style: "Think about... belting a new tunic with your husband's old tie" and "Think about...making your creative side your outside." The campaign was inspired by the maxims published by legendary fashion editor Diana Vreeland in her "Why Don't You..." column for Harper's Bazaar magazine.

The designers created a witty visual corollary for the campaign. The "Think About..." logo complements the black and white squares of the Saks Fifth Avenue identity, previously designed by Pentagram, as well as the right angles and modularity of the identity's grid-based design. Each of the ten letters in "Think About..." is given its own block in the logo. These in turn correspond to ten individual printed catalogs, each in the shape of its block. The letters on the catalog covers are reversed out of fun, simple black and white illustrations of collected items, like shoes (the "B," for "Think about...Banning Boring" catalog), watches and jewelry ("K," for "Think about...Karats", and buttons ("O," for "Think about...Occasionally Outdressing Others.").

Banning Boring.

ALEXANDER McQUEEN

THINK ABOUT...
Nixing Normal

SIMPLE TONE

Project _ Simple Tone Brand Promotion Design
Design Agency _ Shenyang Art Inspiration Design Consultant
Design _ Zhang Lin
Client _ Guangzhou Tone Fahsion Company

As a branch of Tone Fashion, Simple Tone is a fashion brand mainly for Women's dressing. The brand style highlights ladies's maturity, vogue and personality by the application of plain colours such as black, grey and white.

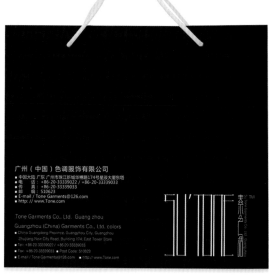

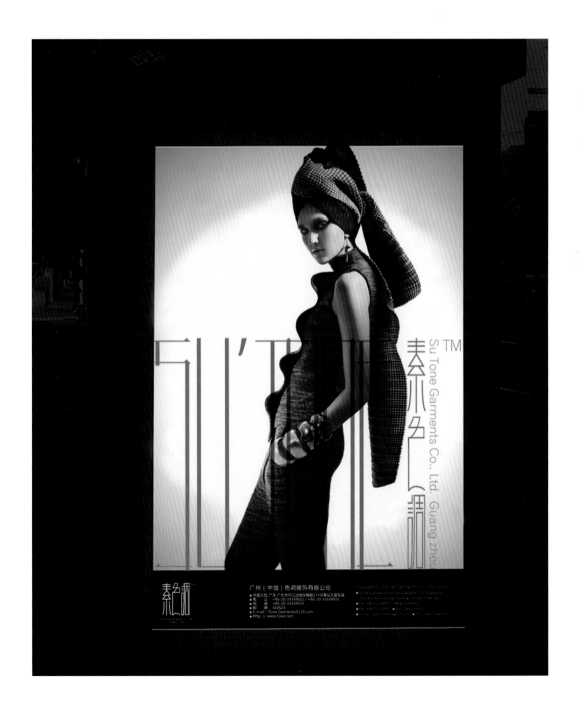

Project _ Freigaenger Corporate Design
Design Agency _ Raum Mannheim
Design _ Frank Hoffmann
Photography _ OPM Fotografie
Client _ Freigaenger Fashion Label

Freigaenger is a small fashion label producing
exclusive clothing. We developed a corporate identity,
including concepts for photography and advertising,
and designed posters, style-cards and a website
for promotion. We also designed a stand for the
fashion fair "blickfang".

FREIGAENGER

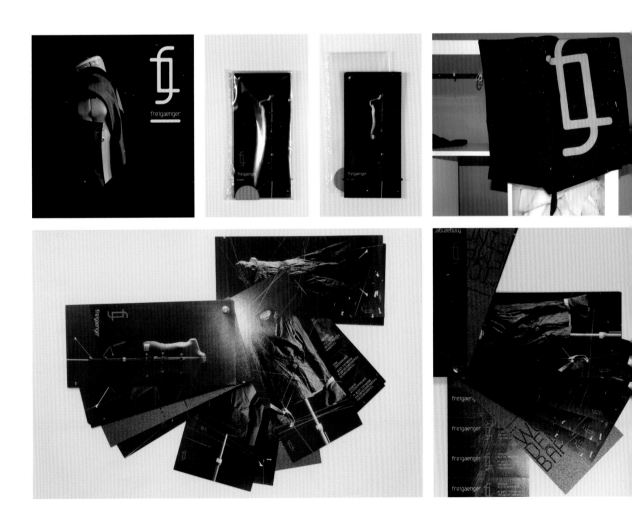

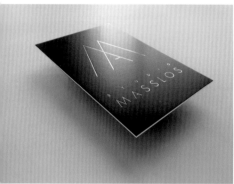

Project _ Masslos Corporate Design
Design Agency _ Raum Mannheim
Design _ Frank Hoffmann
Client _ Masslos

Masslos is a shop selling clothes and accessories.
It is small, refined and individual. We developed a
corporate identity including a logo, signage, interior
design and printed matter.

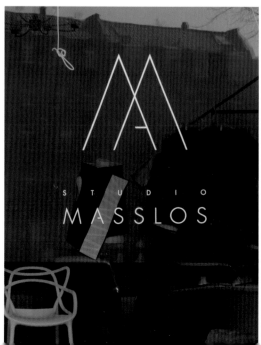

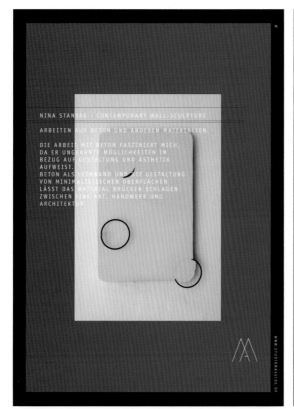

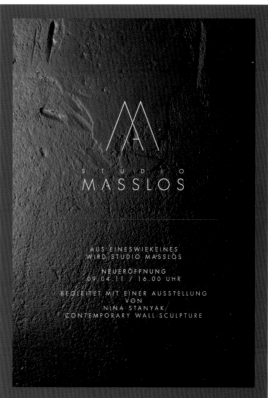

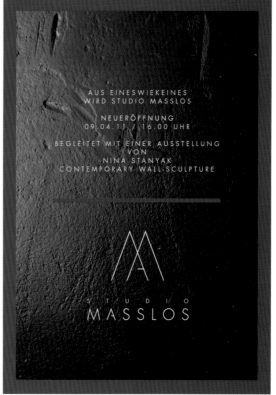

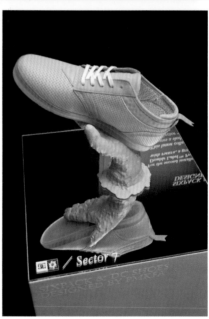

Project _ Sixpack France & DC Shoes
Design Agency _ PMKFA
Client _ Sixpack France & DC Shoes

The type for the collaboration slogan "Six Feet Ahead" is based on how letter shapes would look like if made in soft plastic and exposed to extreme heat. Bending and twisting the once straight letters turns into organic shapes not dissimilar to roots. The thick embroidery make the two-dimensional original graphic come to life, resembling of the images I had in my head when drawing it. The colours match the shoes with it's grey and sober exterior and vivid inside, here made up by purple satin fabric.

PMKFA was asked to design two pair of shoes from the DC Shoes "Life" collection and what you can see here is the PMKFA version of "Sector 7" & "Admiral". What I wanted to achieve was a grey and sober shoe on the outside with a vibrant inside and bottom. The ribbon on the heal states the name of PMKFA, DC and Sixpack on the left and on the right it tells the bragging slogan of the line "Six feet ahead".

SIXPACK FRANCE &
DC SHOES

CULTURE &
PROMOTION

Project _ King Bansah
Design Agency _ Deutsche & Japaner
Design _ Julian Zimmermann
Photography _ Mirka Laura Severa
Client _ King Bansah

King Bansah is an African King. He lives and works in
Ludwigshafen, Germany as a car mechanic and governs
his people from there. King Bansah does a lot of activities
and performances to collect money for his aid projects. He
is a singer and a guest in TV-shows. The new corporate
design should underline his authenticity which is essential
for his activities. The exotic and royal look is expressed on
the printed matters through golden hot foil embossing on
black and chamois-coloured uncoated paper. The story of
the old emblem was kept and redesigned with the edged
and primal shapes of the woven clothes of the Ewe people.

KING BANSAH

Project _ VASCA Corporate Design
Design Agency _ Raum Mannheim
Design _ Frank Hoffmann
Client _ VASCA

VASCA is a musician. He asked us to develop a corporate design, including logo, posters and a CD cover for his latest release.

Project _ OPM Corporate Design
Design Agency _ Raum Mannheim
Design _ Frank Hoffmann
Photography _ OPM Fotografie
Client _ OPM Fotografie

OPM is a photographer. We developed a corporate identity that plays with his photographs and the three letters in his name. We designed stationery, a website and posters to promote the brand.

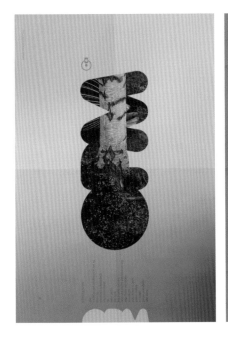

Project _ Spring / Summer 2011 Presentation Collateral
Design Agency _ RoAndCo
Creative Direction _ Roanne Adams
Design _ Tadeu Magalhães
Client _ Honor

Honor, a high-end women's luxury brand, wanted to create
something unique and luxurious for the launch of their brand.
We pulled inspiration from 1960s French films, Le Ballon Rouge
and Belle Du Jour, to help establish Honor's collection image.
Inspired by all things Parisian, the show invitation came in a
box along with gourmet macarons, which created a buzz in the
fashion community and a large turnout at the show.

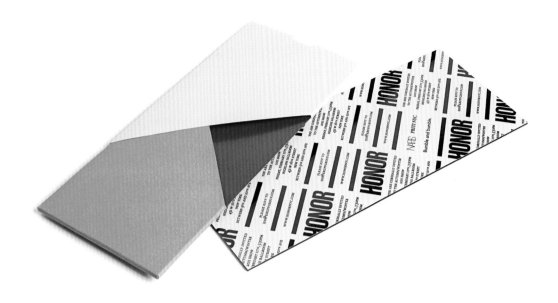

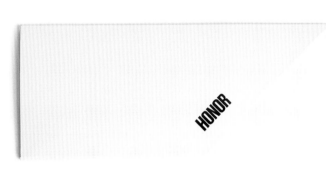

Project _ Force of Love
Design Agency _ JOYN:VISCOM
Design _ NIKE CHINA

Invitation and gift design for Nike Force of Love at 706 space, Beijing. In the 1980s, Nike Air Force 1 opened an era. What did the Chinese young people do at that time? Tapes, sandbags, chalk and whistles. It's the typical memory of sports for the 1980s. The design concept is to take part in the sports by the sympathetic response to emotion.

NIKE CHINA
FORCE OF LOVE

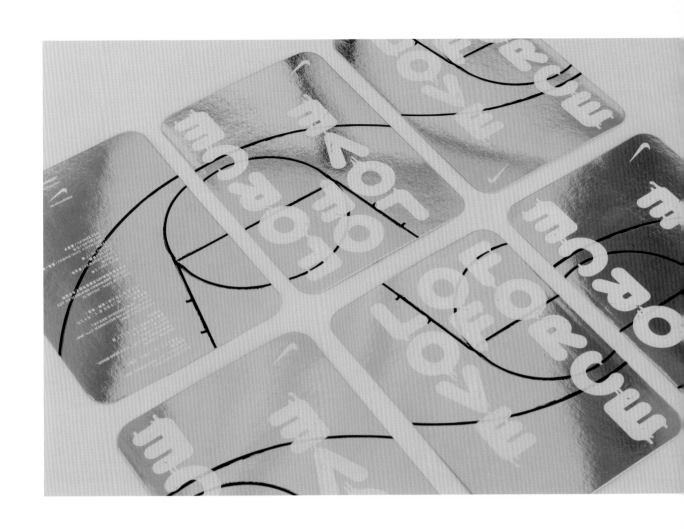

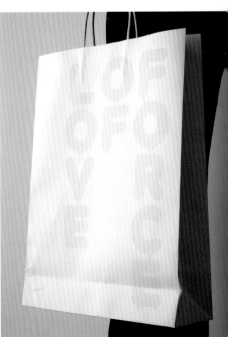

Project _ Victory Night
Design Agency _ JOYN:VISCOM
Design _ NIKE CHINA

JOYN: VISCOM designed materials for the celebration
of "Victory Night" after the Olympic Games.

NIKE CHINA
VICTORY NIGHT

Project _ No Finishing Lines
Design Agency _ JOYN:VISCOM
Design _ NIKE CHINA

JOYN:VISCOM designed the Nike event invitation for the celebration of "the way to victory, Nike innovation 30 anniversary".

NIKE CHINA
NO FINISHING LINES

NIKE CHINA
NIKE 100

Project _ NIKE 100
Design Agency _ JOYN:VISCOM
Design _ NIKE CHINA

INNOV8 creative salon was held in NIKE 706 Space. Tinker Hatfield, the Vice President of Nike, shared his rich experiences of product design with the visitors. The visual identity of Nike 100 told the history of Nike. JOYN:VISCOM designed the visual production materials and commemorative items.

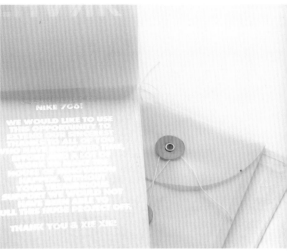

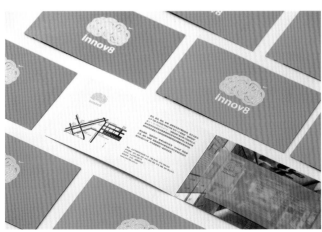

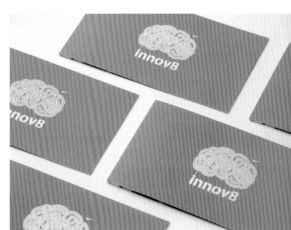

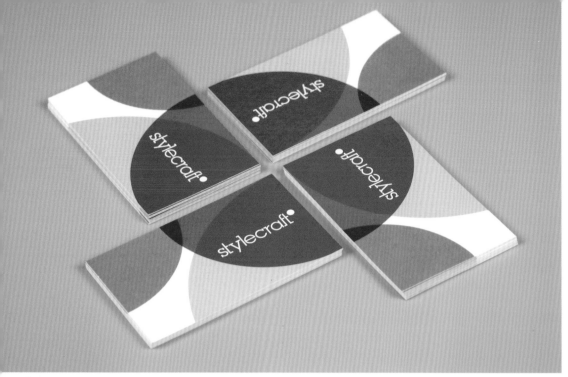

STYLECRAFT

Project _ Stylecraft Brand Development
Design Agency _ THERE Design
Design _ Paul Taboure, Jon Zhu
Client _ Stylecraft

Stylecraft is an international contemporary furniture company with a portfolio of distinct brands such as Arper, Walter Knoll and Tacchini. We were asked to revitalise the existing brand identity collateral and inject a more vibrant, engaging and flexible brand extension system. Taking the existing circular symbol from their well-known logo as a starting point, we created a library of complimentary geometric graphics that more closely reflects the company's brand personality. The outcome brought the brand to life, injecting a dynamic, fun, personable and high design aesthetic result.

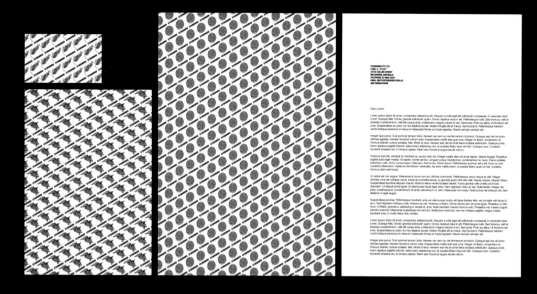

Project _ Studio Bird Visual Identity
Design Agency _ 3 Deep Design
Art Direction _ 3 Deep Design
Design _ 3 Deep Design
Client _ Studio Bird

Matthew Bird is founder & director of Studio Bird; a design practice delivering innovative projects that combine interior & architectural solutions. As a young practice within the Australian architectural landscape, Studio Bird is incredibly unique. It is through the process of research, with a focus on resourcefulness and rigor, that the practices projects are, to date, exceptional manifestations of the clients brief within the context of site, budget and social & environmental sensitivities. 3 Deep Design was engaged by Studio Bird to establish a visual identity and creative positioning that captured the essence and personality of the practice.

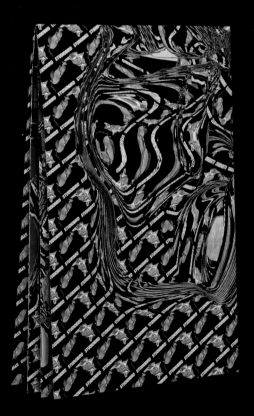

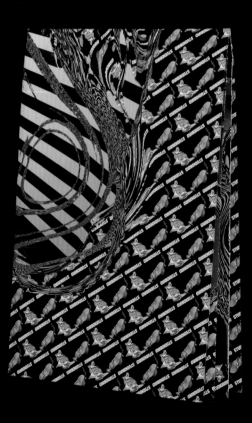

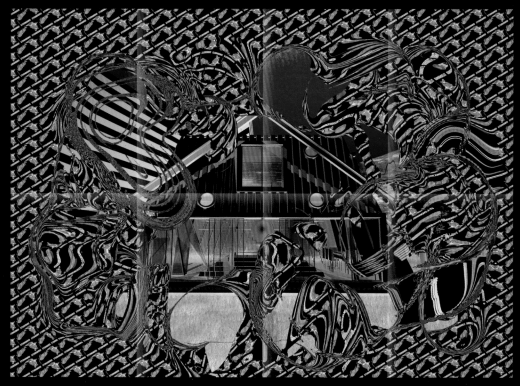

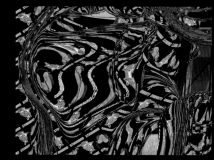
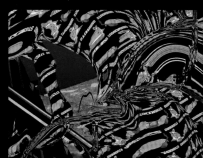
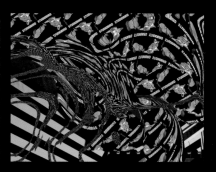

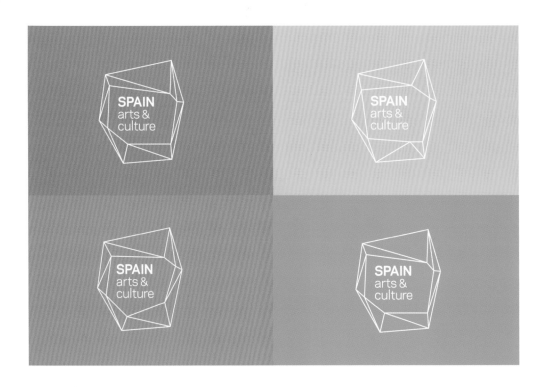

Project _ SPAIN arts & culture
Design Agency _ Toormix
Design _ Oriol Armengou, Ferran Mitjans
Client _ Embassy of Spain

Spain arts & culture is a new brand born to reflect all the expressions of Spain, and convey the cultural variety of the country. The project includes the identity, the stationery and the first program with all the events across the US.

An evolving stone, therefore, is the new symbol that helps us reach the United States from the other side of the Atlantic, a stone that moves, almost alive, that evolves constantly and shows new expressions with each step it takes. We present to you the new brand that represents Spanish culture. It is a gem that wants to be discovered and admired, because many engravers have worked on it and others continue to give it shape. There is much to be discovered.

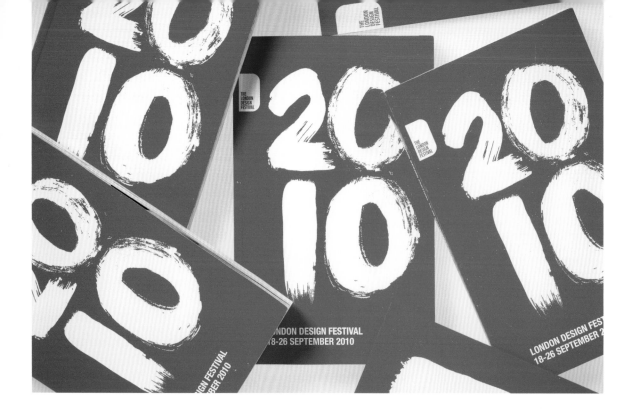

Project _ London Design Festival
Design Agency _ Pentagram Design
Design _ Domenic Lippa, Beatrice Blumenthal
Client _ London Design Festival

The London Design Festival is an annual event that in 2010 ran from 18 to 26 September. During the week over 200 events and installations took place across the capital reflecting the widest possible range of design interests. For the fourth year running Domenic Lippa and his team worked to create a new visual identity ensuring that the Festival brand has visibility across all of its disparate elements.

This year's mark is all about creativity reacting against the formality of the previous year's clean typographic approach. Using an intuitive graphic solution led towards a hand drawn painted alphabet created by Beatrice Blumenthal. The alphabet is used to express some impressive facts and figures for the Festival in bold hand drawn figures for instance 300,000 visitors, 200 events and London being the number 1 city for design. These facts and figures are used to adorn the guide as well as T-shirts, bags, advertisements and the website.

In addition to the main look and feel the team have created a VIP solution using a black palette for invitations.

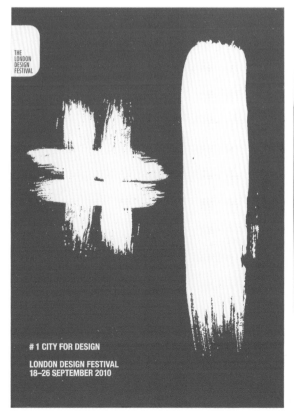

1 CITY FOR DESIGN
LONDON DESIGN FESTIVAL 2010

1 CITY FOR DESIGN

LONDON DESIGN FESTIVAL
18–26 SEPTEMBER 2010

STUART HAYGARTH
MAX LAMB
OSKAR ZIETA
CONTEMPORARY BRITISH SILVER
MICHAEL ANASTASSIADES
26 TREASURES
JOHNSON BANKS
ONKAR KULAR & NOAM TORAN
KIKIT VISUOSONIC
ISTITUTO MARANGONI
HIDDEN V&A IPOD TOUR

20
10

Project _ Turnstyle Promotional Bags
Design Agency _ Turnstyle
Design _ Madeleine Eiche
Client _ Turnstyle

We try to make all our promotional materials unique, memorable and / or humorous. For our portfolio mailer, we sort of deconstructed a FedEx-style mailer. The plastic pocket houses interchangeable portfolio postcards, while the screen-printed chipboard affords protection and rigidity. A bonus perforated handle allows you to carry it around with pride. Without overstating the importance of environmental impact, the message on our canvas bags – "This is neither plastic, nor English" – is a tongue-in-cheek nod to other didactic bags out there.

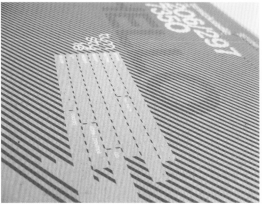

Project _ Stylecraft & Arper 10 / 10 Branding
Design Agency _ THERE Design
Design _ Paul Taboure, Jon Zhu
Client _ Stylecraft

Stylecraft is an international contemporary furniture company with a portfolio of distinct furniture brands. They approached us to help launch 10 new furniture products from renowned Italian furniture maker Arper,whilst also simultaneously celebrating their 10-year business partnership. The event consisted of a series of VIP Invitation only sessions targeting design industry professionals. We created an experiential event with bespoke product information and branded acrylic signage, as well as "fun" take home souvenirs including posters, DVD packs and badges.

STYLECRAFT & ARPER
10 RANGES CELEBRATING
10 YEARS TOGETHER

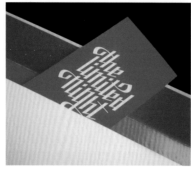

THE LIMITED NIGHT PARTY

Project _ The Limited Night Party Identity
Design Agency _ kissmiklos
Design _ Miklós Kiss
Photography _ Miklós Kiss, Poster's photo by Bettina Gál

Identity and slogan concept for a pop party series.

Project _ Nike SB X Gift Team Movie Premiere
Design Agency _ Nike Brand Design China
Design Direction _ Mike Delaney
Design _ Queenie He, James Qu
Client _ Nike

Nike SB hosts a Christmas themed premiere party to present the first skate film in China to the local skate community.

Taking inspiration from authentic skate material and the skate team's name GIFT, we created a deconstructed skate ramp as screening seating. To indulge the X'mas theme, we used hundreds of gift boxes to create a unique exhibition space and guest can take the boxes away after party, they are full of SB goodies.

NIKE SB
X GIFT TEAM
MOVIE PREMIERE

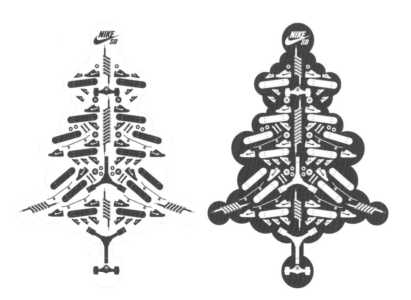

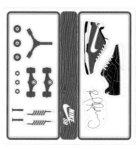

Project _ POMY
Design Agency _ TYMOTE
Client _ POMY

Developed a branding for an artist shop, "POMY",
which collects, showcases, and sells art works
from young designers. Implemented art direction,
shop designing, and project planning.

Êdesu Yan
no
Mise desuYan
=
Pirates
Of
Mise desu
Yan

captain: TYMOTE™

POMY

Project _ Starbucks Coffee Shop
Design Agency _ G.O.D. Ltd.

The first ever Starbucks store in the world to
incorporate a "Bing Sutt" corner - an innovative
concept designed by G.O.D. - that fuses together a
nostalgic retro style with contemporary coffee house.
The design is based on Hong Kong style.

STARBUCKS
COFFEE SHOP

DATE OF THE HEAL

Project _ Date of the Heal
Design _ Yao Ye, Li Xibin
Client _ Lining

It's a theme campaign and new product release for Lining Sportwear.

YII

Project _ Yii Identity
Design Agency _ Onion Design Associates
Director _ Janett Wang
Creative Direction _ Andrew Wong
Design _ Karen Tsai
Client _ Taiwan Craft Research and Development Institute

A very subtle and minimal exhibition Identity commissioned by Taiwan Craft Research and Development Institute. Yii - An on going exhibition featuring collaboration works of 15 designers and 20 traditional craftsmen, opening at Milano Triennale this year. Designed by Onion.

"Yii" (易) - pronounced as the letter E - Taking from the classic text I-Ching (易经), also known as the Book of Changes. The logo mark design, as requested by creative director Gijs Bakker (co-founder of Droog Design) , need to be very simple and not looking too logo. We decided that a pure minimal typographic approach would work. Typeface "Avant Garde Extra Light" was selected for its geometrical simplicity. We modified the strokes and spacing as a subtly reference to a Trigram figure marking from the bagua (八卦) symbol; mimicking one of the eight possible trigrams of the I-Ching, ☰ (The solid line represents yang. The open line represents yin).

ADIDAS MI ORIGINALS
x WINDOWS 7
x DOROPHY TANG
EXHIBITION

Project _ Adidas mi Originals x Windows 7 x Dorophy Tang Exhibition
Design Agency _ Adidas, Windows 7, Dorophy Tang
Design _ Dorophy Tang
Client _ Adidas Originals, Windows 7

In August 2010, adidas teamed up with the world famous software company Microsoft, started a project for Window 7 with Dorophy Tang – the long term partnership with adidas. Dorophy designed 7 different characteristics of her famous icon Shopping Baby which inspired by Window 7, these 7 characters were painted on 7 adidas classic models and have an exhibition in adidas original concept store Hong Kong, China. The exhibition was then brought to Beijing adidas Concept Store in Sanlitun Village.

Project _ Kick Discovery Asia Tour Exhibition
Design _ Dorophy Tang
Client _ Adidas originals, Epson Printers, Windows 7 (Microsoft)

Kick Discovery Asia Tour Exhibition, Beijing, Hong Kong & Taipei. Applying a new form of Qing Hua Ci style on Shopping Babies figures with concepts of adidas originals classic shoes models.

KICK DISCOVERY ASIA TOUR EXHIBITION

KICKS DISCOVERY BEIJING by DOROPHY TANG

Project _ Sony PlayStation GDC 2009
Design Agency _ Exposure
Creative Direction _ Tom Phillips
Design _ Irwin Matutina
Client _ Sony PlayStation

For the 2009 GDC conference we designed and produced a trade show booth concept based around the brand theme of "Community". Creative direction centered around conversation and was executed as interactive speech bubbles, incorporating quotes from the language of the gaming and social communities to create a unified method of presenting forthcoming hardware and game titles.

We also executed a creatively themed "Blow Up" party, with live headline performance from Janelle Monae, with a supporting cast of DJ's. The event environment consisted of branded inflatable objects integrated into the venue and surrounding area, alongside indoor and exterior projections of a commissioned short film on "inflatable living".

SONY PLAYSTATION

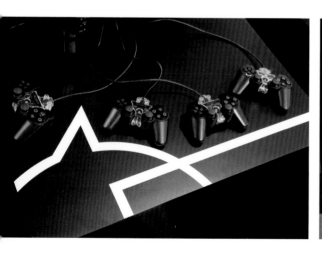

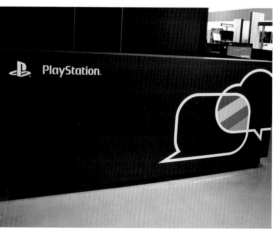

Project _ The Museum of Modern Art Identity
Design Agency _ Pentagram Design with The Museum of Modern Art
Design _ Paula Scher, Julia Hoffmann
Client _ The Museum of Modern Art

The Museum of Modern Art (MoMA) possesses one of the most recognizable logotypes of any cultural institution in the world. While the logo is iconic in itself, the museum needed a comprehensive institutional identity that would carry the spirit of MoMA across multiple platforms. The designers created a focused, organized and flexible identity system that supports program material in print, web and environmental applications. The system employs prominent use of the MoMA logo as a graphic device. An appropriate scale and careful cropping were developed to make the identity more powerful and cohesive, and to create an attitude that modernizes the institution's image. A strong grid has been established for the uniform placement of elements. Images of artworks appear whole or are cropped for effect. The images are paired with the logotype, which has a consistent vertical placement similar to the signage on the museum's façade.

THE MUSEUM OF
MODERN ART

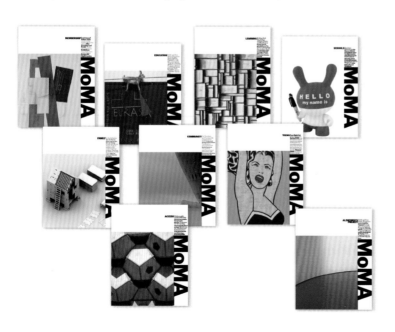

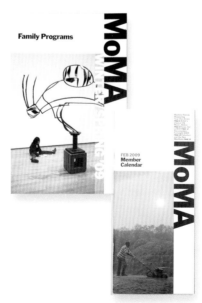

24-25

Project _ 24-25
Design Agency _ Sagmeister inc.
Art direction _ Stefan Sagmeister
Design _ Joe Shouldice, Richard The
Client _ Museum Plaza

24-25 variable identity changes with the art that is exhibited at any given time within the Museum Plaza Complex.

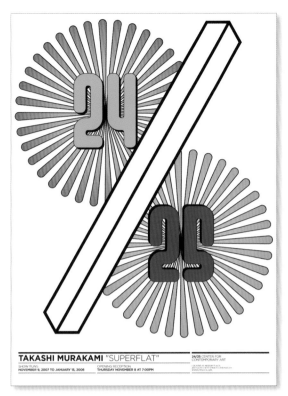

TAKASHI MURAKAMI "SUPERFLAT"

SHOW RUNS
NOVEMBER 9, 2007 TO JANUARY 15, 2008

OPENING RECEPTION
THURSDAY NOVEMBER 8 AT 7:00PM

24/25 CENTER FOR
CONTEMPORARY ART

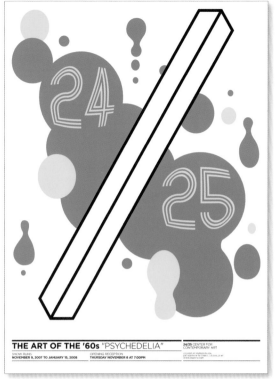

THE ART OF THE '60s "PSYCHEDELIA"

SHOW RUNS
NOVEMBER 9, 2007 TO JANUARY 15, 2008

OPENING RECEPTION
THURSDAY NOVEMBER 8 AT 7:00PM

24/25 CENTER FOR
CONTEMPORARY ART

Project _ Global Competition for Shenzhen City Logo Design
Design Agency _ DESIGNDO BRAND DESIGN CONSULTING
ORGANIZATION
Creative Direction _ jj.lee, Long Gang
Art Direction _ Meng Yuanhan
Design _ Meng Yuanhan, jj.lee, Long Gang
Typography _ Meng Yuanhan
Copywriter _ Meng Yuanhan
Photography _ Meng Yuanhan
Illustration _ Meng Yuanhan
Client _ Shenzhen Government

As an international city, Shenzhen decided to collect her city logo
from all over the world. We did the visual identity for the event to
highlight the dynamic characteristics of the city. The main graphics
is formed by fluorescent green lines. The free-form identity conveys
the active image and reflects the features of Shenzhen city.

GLOBAL
COMPETITION
FOR SHENZHEN CITY
LOGO DESIGN

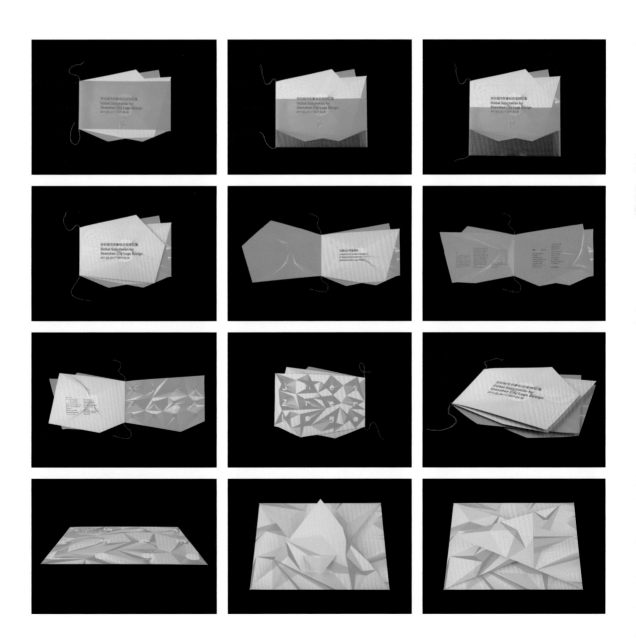

Project _ The 2nd Celebration of Shenzhen Sidagao Porcelain
Design Agency _ DESIGNDO BRAND DESIGN CONSULTING ORGANIZATION
Creative Direction _ jj.lee, Long Gang
Art Direction _ Meng Yuanhan
Design _ jj.lee, Long Gang, Meng Yuanhan
Typography _ jj.lee
Copywriter _ Long Gang
Illustration _ jj.lee
Client _ Shenzhen Sidagao Porcelain Industry Center

It's the 2nd Celebration of Shenzhen Sidagao Porcelain. The theme is unbounded on "Porcelain" imagination. It's a platform for exchange by using Porcelain as the materials to freely create appliques. The concept is designing the font by the application of appliques. The various periods of porcelain patterns are the basic elements of the unique fond design.

THE 2ND CELEBRATION OF SHENZHEN SIDAGAO PORCELAIN

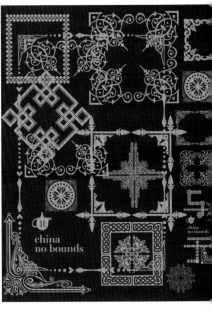

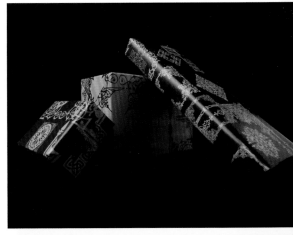

Project _ Beijing "Shenzhen Culture Week" – Celebration of the 30th Shenzhen Anniversary, Shenzhen Graphic Design Review Invitation Exhibition
Design Agency _ 5W.1H Brand Solution Ltd
Design _ Heng Aik-soon, Wilson
Credits _ Heng Aik-soon, Wilson, LW.JIE, Gary Choi, 5W.1H Teams
Client _ Propaganda Department of the CPC Shenzhen Municipal Committee, Tourism Bureau of Shenzhen City, Association of Shenzhen Literary and Art Circles, Fine Arts College of Tsinghua University, Shenzhen Graphic Design Association

30 After 30

30 years before: Deng Xiaoping drew a "circle" on the map and created a Special Economic Zone called Shenzhen in 1980s.

30 years at this moment: the "circle" of Shenzhen, the "circle" of China, the "circle" of the world.

The next 30 years: the "circle" of Shenzhen in future will influence the world.

Celebration of the 30th Shenzhen Anniversary during Beijing "Shenzhen Culture Week" held in Fine Arts College of Tsinghua University, Beijing. By GDC Graphic Design in China, the history of Shenzhen graphic design was reviewed. The 30-year reform achievement was displayed by the poster invitation exhibition. And "30 After 30" is an activity for the future of Shenzhen to express the imagination of the future.

30 AFTER 30

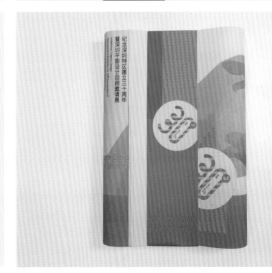

Project _ Inspiration Design - "Type Play" Promotion
Design Agency _ Art Inspiration Design Consultant
Design _ Zhang Lin
Client _ Type Play

As a branch of Art Inspiration Design Consultant, Type Play specializes in creative design and research of Chinese characters. It smartly conveys the happiness of Chinese font design. A series of promotion materials is designed in modern style.

TYPE PLAY

ABCDEFGHIJKMN
OPQRSTUVWXYZ
0123456789/@%!?&()""..-+_

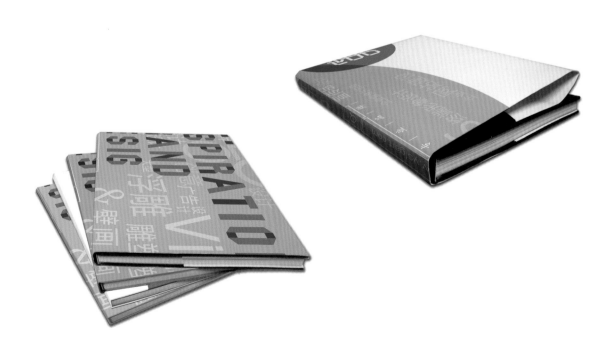

 LATVIA EXPO PAVILION

Project _ Visual Identity of Latvia for World EXPO 2010
Design Agency _ Asketic
Credits _ Krisjanis Jukumsons, Aigars Mamis, Mikelis Bastiks
Design _ Latvia EXPO Pavilion, Aerodium

Moving away from the old and worn-out traditional patterns, we have taken a different look at our nation and ignited a new spirit of happiness into Latvia's visual identity to help present the country in a fresh way according to the overall concept of Latvia's pavilion - Technology of Happiness.

Project _ Spiral
Design Agency _ Thonik
Design _ Spiral Art Center, Tokyo
Client _ Spiral

Spiral is an arts institution in central Tokyo. Thonik was asked to design their corporate identity campaign and to mark the 25th anniversary of the institution. The new design is based on the existing modernist logo by Masayoshi Nakajo. The circles in the design symbolize the various activities and projects of the institute. The transformation of the logo is associated with the plan of the building that consists of a circle and a rectangle. The new style is in line with the strategy of Thonik for the past 3 years to create new and flexible graphic systems from an existing font.

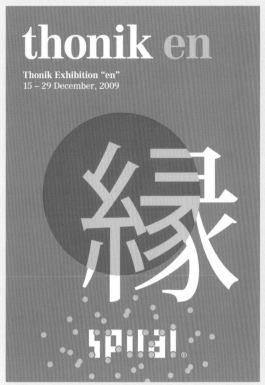

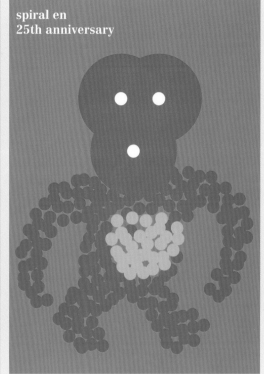

INDEX

...,staat creative agency

...,staat creative agency is an international creative agency based in Amsterdam, the Netherlands.

Set up in 2000, ...,staat creative agency established itself as an independent world player. Staat works with local heroes and global brands. The agency exists of original thinkers, who know no limits and deliver fully-integrated branding, from strategy to concept to design. With passion, Staat turns the everyday into the iconic, creating work that touches people.

www.staatamsterdam.nl

p.134

&Larry

&Larry begins every project by putting the name of our client or creative partner before our own. This spirit of collaboration and mutual respect is reflected in the thinking that goes into each piece of work.

We believe that art and design shouldn't exist in separate vacuums. Be it commercial or experimental, &Larry always seeks to create works that are honest, functional and expressive beyond aesthetics.

The studio has adopted the Eames motto of "Take your pleasure seriously" and examples of this philosophy can be seen in a diverse body of work from posters and print campaigns to our series of Singapore-inspired art objects.

www.andlarry.com

p.054-055, 094-095, 110-111, 168-169

2x4

2x4 is a collaborative group of creative directors, writers, and designers founded in 1994 by partners Michael Rock, Susan Sellers, and Georgianna Stout. With cutting-edge projects in virtually all graphic media-print, web, motion graphics, and environmental design, 2x4's trademark approach heavily emphasizes critical thinking and research. Known for intellectual content and explorations of rhetorical meaning, many of 2x4's projects question the nature of design and are as much about the thinking process behind each work as the finished product. This ideology, based on an almost algorithmic approach, is the foundation for 2x4's pioneering model for design, one that makes process the product." Joseph Rosa, Curator, Art Institute of Chicago.

www.2x4.org

p.162-163

3 Deep Design

3 Deep Design is a design and image agency based in Australia with representation in New York, Tokyo and Europe. For over 15 years the practice has crafted programmes for the finest galleries, private clients and organisations around the world, notably Steven Klein & Madonna for Louis Vuitton, Six Scents, The Australian Ballet, Seven New York, Toni Maticevski & Materialbyproduct. 3 Deep's clients are discerning and appreciate emotionally and intellectually driven design

www.3deep.com.au

p.060-061, 204-205

Alfio Mazzei

Alfio Mazzei graduated in visual communication at the SUPSI university (2002) in Lugano, Switzerland. After the school he worked for more than one year at the for Giacomo Spazio at Air Studio, Milan. He moved then to Amsterdam where he lived and worked as a freelance until summer 2005, year in which he moved to south Spain. Since 2005 he is working as a freelance for some studios and agencies, and in 2007 start to collaborate with CCRZ studio. At the moment works partly as an independent designer and partly as a freelance.

www.fs52.com

p.034-035

Anagrama

We are a specialized brand development and positioning agency providing creative solutions for any type of project. Besides our history and experience with brand development, we are also experts in the design and development of objects, spaces and multimedia projects.

We create the perfect balance between a design boutique, focusing on the development of creative pieces paying attention to the smallest of details, and a business consultancy providing solutions based on the analysis of tangible data to generate best fit applications.

A well managed and positioned brand represents a powerful asset for the company's total value. It is a sales tool and a client loyalty promoter.

www.anagrama.com

p.016-017, 144

Apartment One

Apartment One is a brand media and design company that gives voice to the truth, presence and power of your brand. We find strength in creative partnerships, excitement at the birth of a new venture, and passion in the service of a greater good.

www.apartmentone.net

p.114-115

Artless Inc

Established in 2000. "artless" is an independently owned design studio, by Shun Kawakami, based in Tokyo, Japan.

The activities are in the framework and language of design, corporate identity, brand development and design solutions.

www.artless.co.jp

p.135

Asketic

We are a full-service design shop based in Riga and Sand Francisco. We appreciate purity, simplicity, and nice people.

http://asketic.com/

p.242-243

Berg

Berg is an independent UK based ideas studio. We design seamlessly across a wide range of inter-disciplinary media including design for print, screen and the environment.

We have an international reputation for consistently applying innovation, imagination, and sound commercial values.

At the heart of all our activities is a collaborative process by which we work closely with clients and industry professionals to create solutions which are considered, engaging and effective.

www.bergstudio.co.uk

p.022, 079, 148-149

BLOW

BLOW is a Hong Kong based design studio founded by Ken Lo in 2010. Specialized in branding, identities, packaging, environmental graphics, print, publications and website design, we provide clients with mind-blowing design in simple and bold approach that helps the brand to stand out in the crowd.

www.blow.hk

p.026-027

Bobchen Design Office Hangzhou

Bob Chen was born in Zhoushan, Zhejiang, in 1979. He graduated from a major of fashion design. He established Bobchen Design Office in 2004. His studio specialized in visual art, space, furniture and comprehensive applications. He is active in related design fields including lecture, education and exhibitions.

www.bobchen.cn

p.056-057, 088-089, 174-175

Bond Creative Agency

We are a creative agency focused on branding and design. We create and renew brands.

Bond is founded and run by designers. We work for clients who value creative and practical ideas. We demonstrate our expertise through our work rather than talking, because design is, first and foremost, a craft for us. We design, visualize and define brands in a way that help companies differentiate themselves from the competition. This can mean creating brand identities, branded environments, packaging, experiential web services or advertising. We are agile and designer-driven. Our clients appreciate working directly with the designers.

www.bond-agency.com

p.010-011

Bravo

Bravo Company is a creatively led, independent design studio based in Singapore. We work with a variety of individuals and organizations to deliver considered and engaging design. We specialize in identity & brand development, printed communications & art direction.

www.bravo-company.info

p.106-107

C100 Purple Haze

C100 Purple Haze is a Munich based multidisciplinary design consultancy founded by Christian Hundertmark (C100) and Clemens Baldermann (Purple Haze). The studio's diverse output included projects for miscellaneous public and private clients on a variety of national and international projects including expertise in conception, art direction, typography, design and illustration. Specialised in delivering inventive and precise visual solutions we approach each project with enthusiasm, dedicated hands, and an individual style which is evident in our works.

www.c100purplehaze.com

p.172

Checkland Kindleysides

In the three decades since we began designing, it is perhaps not surprising that we've grown. With experience we have gained both creative diversity, and an ability to create work that is aesthetically, physically and commercial successful.

We have always been careful to hang on to what we believe makes designers truly resourceful; time-honed skills, natural talent and enquiring minds. We apply ourselves totally on every projects, large or small, and we fuel our creativity through knowledge. Collaborative by nature, we will lead, steer, guide, inspire, and take the leap when it comes to our clients. Importantly, we will also listen. It is this ability to pause that has created so many long-standing relationships.

www.checklandkindleysides.com

p.133

DEMIAN CONRAD DESIGN

Created in 2007, the DEMIAN CONRAD DESIGN is based in Lausanne, Switzerland. Working mainly in the cultural field and the leisure industry, the studio lends its expertise to everything related to events communication and visual identity. Multi-disciplinary, the studio favours a "lateral thinking" approach with the aim of finding creative, destabilising solutions and forms of avant-garde, cutting-edge, hard-hitting communication. Projects successfully carried out by the studio include the identity of the Gabbani brand, the campaign for the Lausanne Underground Film Festival, the innovative approach of the Blackswan foundation as well as projects for conferences such as TED and the Forum des 100.

www.demianconrad.com

p.112-113

DESIGNDO BRAND DESIGN CONSULTING ORGANIZATION

DESIGNDO BRAND DESIGN CONSULTING ORGANIZATION is a group of designers who share the same ambitions and purposes. It is also the partners who share brand experience together. We advocate a five-sense experience as the core of the unique point of view and create a unique brand concept to reach the real life and true design. Thanks to years' in-depth brand exploration, we offer our perfect brand marketing solutions for our customers.

www.dd-brand.com

p.234-235

Deutsche & Japaner

Deutsche & Japaner studio was initiated in 2008 and offers expertise in various disciplines, such as graphic design, product design, interior design, illustration and scenography as well as conceptual creation and strategic brand escort.

The studio focuses on communication, regards less of its physical condition, environmental, haptical or visual, but always in regard of sustainable experiences.

www.deutscheundjapaner.com

p.190-191

Dorophy Tang

Dorophy Tang, a product designer / an illustrator, was born and raised in Hong Kong, China. She was badly influenced with the fusion-culture in Hong Kong, China. The mixture of traditional

Chinese blue and white arts plus the modern western street style became her signatured style. She calls it the Modern Qing Hua Ci. She also draws chubby Chinese babies, called Shopping Babies which are illustrations in traditional-Chinese-influenced style plus recent-trend-culture of young people. Dorophy was famed of collaborating with some famous brands like adidas originals, Epson, Nikon, Lomography, etc. She has been awarded by Perspective Magazine's 40 under 40: Asia's Top Young Designers in 2009.

http://allaboutdorophytang.blogspot.com
p.226-227

e-Types

e-Types is a strategic brand and design agency that moves companies and organizations forward through identity. Knowledge and skill is key in our clear and concise design solution – across all media platforms. We immerse ourselves in art projects and our type foundry Playtype[TM].

We gravitate between highly accomplished commercial clients, solid public institutions and the more off-centre and trendy - allowing us to retain our dynamics and avoid being locked into one particular segment or type of client. We believe this provides us with an edge that we can apply to all our clients since the different segments and industries constantly overlap and inspire each other.

www.e-types.com
p.012-013, 164-165

Enav Tomer

A Graphic Designer from Israel. I recently graduated from Shenkar College of Engineering and Design.

www.enavtomer.com
p.068-069

Eps51

Eps51 is an internationally working design studio developing conceptual visual solutions for projects of various disciplines ranging from print to web, from brand identity to illustration and photography. Before settling down in Berlin in 2008 the founders Ben Wittner and Sascha Thoma lived and worked in London, Paris, Brussels and Cairo for a while. Eps51 have worked on numerous intercultural projects over the past years, mostly for clients from the cultural field. In 2008 they published the book "Arabesque – Graphic Design from the Arab World and Persia" (Die Gestalten) – the result of a long lasting, intensive research on the Middle Eastern graphic design scene. Clients include Nike, L'Oréal, Ninja Tunes, Art Dubai, Gestalten Publishers ...

www.eps51.com
p.140-141

Exposure

We are a creative agency working with brands to generate good solid ideas. We believe in sparking conversations. Conversations that are shared. With offices in New York, San Francisco and London we work across a wide range of media and disciplines to deliver the good news. We are always glad to provide a point of view. Let us know what you are thinking.

www.exposure.net
p.228-229

Fabio Ongarato Design

Founded in 1992 by partners Fabio Ongarato and Ronnen Goren, based in Australia, Fabio Ongarato Design is renowned for the diversity of its work. The studio takes an open approach to graphic design, operating across a variety of graphic disciplines, from print to exhibitions to advertising. FOD's approach to design reflects their passion for architecture, photography and contemporary art. They work across a variety of fields such as fashion, corporate, arts and architecture deliberately crossing the boundaries between them.

www.fabioongaratodesign.com.au
p.108-109

fg branddesign

Founded in early 2010 fg branddesign is a design agency, base in Stuttgart (Germany), the angency develops holistic brand communication for companies in the field of premium and luxury goods. At fg branddesign the combination of strategic intelligence and creative excellence is considered the crucial factor of successful communication. In its first year the agency was awarded by several international design and media awards.

www.fg-branddesign.com
p.018-019

FORMZOO

Formzoo is a Berlin based collective of young designers and illustrators. We work in modular teams to create the best synergies for each idea. We believe in thoughtful, honest concepts. Told in metaphors, simple but meaningful. Markus Guenther is co-founder of FORMZOO and independent designer and illustrator.

www.formzoo.com
p.052-053

Fujimoto Gumi

Fujimoto Gumi is a Nagoya based design agency.

www.fujimoto-gumi.com
p.132

Glasfurd & Walker

Established in early 2007, Glasfurd & Walker offer multi-disciplinary, conceptual and design services and innovative brand communication and design solutions. With each project presenting new challenges and demanding unique outcomes, strategic, idea driven design is key to their approach. The studio services include, but are not limited to: identity and brand design, art direction and design for print and online communication, signage & installation, exhibition design and packaging.

www.glasfurdandwalker.com
p.090-091, 126-127

G.O.D.

Since 1996, Good of Desire has been producing designs that are inspired by Hong Kong China's unique culture. By fusing the new with the old, the east with the west, G.O.D. is Hong Kong China's modern identity for future generations.

www.god.com.hk
p.220-221

Heine / Lenz / Zizka

The design agency Heine / Lenz / Zizka focusses on visual communication. We help our clients to define the core of their brand in order to communicate successfully - analog and digital. At our offices in Frankfurt and Berlin about 25 employees create products, corporate images and communication concepts that bring brands to life.

The agency was founded in 1989 by Achim Heine, Michael Lenz and Peter Zizka. For several years Heine / Lenz / Zizka is among the top 10 in the ranking of creative design agencies in Germany.

www.hlz.de
p.014-015

Heng Aik-soon, Wilson

Heng Aik-soon, Wilson is an Asian Chinese Designer who was born in Malaysia and graduated from RMIT University, Melbourne, Australia in 1988. Having over a decade of experience in renowned international advertising agencies and brand solution companies in Singapore (DIA, based in London - Europe top 10) and Hong Kong, China (Head of Kan and Lau Design Consultant, Shenzhen), Wilson established his own firm - 5W.1H Brand Solution Ltd in Hong Kong, China since 2005.

The company's scope of business ranges from corporate identity, environmental graphics, literature, packaging design and last but not least, design education. His clientele spans China (The Mainland, Hong Kong & Taiwan), Malaysia and Singapore.

www.5w1hbrand.com
p.154-155, 238-239

Hiromura Masaaki

He was born in Aichi prefecture, in 1954. He entered Tanaka Ikko Design Office in 1977 and established Hiromura Masaaki Design Office in 1988. He won many awards all over the world including JAGDA New Designer Award, N.Y. ADC 9th International Annual Exhibition Silver Award, CS Design Award (Decoration Category Gold Award), SDA Diamond Award, 15th CS Design Award (Sign Category Gold Award), KU/KAN Award 2008, Mainichi Design Awards 2008

www.hiromuradesign.com

p.023, 070-071

HORT

HORT began its inhabitance back in 1994, under the previous stage name of EIKES GRAFISCHER HORT. Who is Eike? Eike is the creator of HORT. HORT - a direct translation of the studio's mission. A creative playground. A place where "work and play" can be said in the same sentence. An unconventional working environment. Once a household name in the music industry. Now, a multi-disciplinary creative hub. Not just a studio space, but an institution devoted to making ideas come to life. A place to learn, a place to grow, and a place that is still growing. Not a client execution tool. HORT has been known to draw inspiration from things other than design.

www.hort.org.uk

p.137, 166-167

Idea With Legs

Design is not just styling, but more an idea with legs.

www.withlegs.com

p.038-039

James Qu

Great China Nike Brand design designer.

www.nike.com

p.160-161, 216-217

JJAAKK

JJAAKK is an independent graphic design studio with a passion for creating work that speaks for itself. Specializing in packaging systems, identities and posters for clients both big and small, JJAAKK strives for design solutions that are bold, fun, intriguing and above all, smart.

www.jjaakk.com

p.070-071

JOYN:VISCOM

JOYN: VISCOM is an independent, multi-disciplinary design studio and communication consultancy based in Beijing, China. The studio aims to experiences, whether they're commissioned client-work or self-initiated projects. By working across diverse disciplines, the studio consistently delivers exclusive, creative and easy-going solutions.

In addition, JOYN: VISCOM produces a wide range of projects, including exhibitions, lectures, publications, and events. All efforts the team has been making are to explore all facets of contemporary visual culture and communications.

www.joynviscom.com

p.196-197

Kila Cheung

Kila Cheung, born in Hong Kong, China, a city best known for its historic traditional and fusion of Chinese and Western culture.

After graduation from HK polytechnic University, Kila is working as a graphic designer. Since Kila was working in commercial design house in the past few years, he found that there were so many rules to tell what kind of design was regarded as great graphic work. But Kila wishes to deviate those rules as he believes great works is something that people never seen before and that's what he is desiring to create.

In 2011 Kila becomes a committee member of the Hong Kong Society of Illustrators. Kila enjoys doing his own design and illustration in his spare time and desires to communicate with others via his works.

www.kilacheung.com

p.142-143

Lin Shaobin Design

Lin Shaobin is a Shantou based creative from Guangdong, China. He is a top ten designer of Guangdong. With eight year's experience, he is the chief designer and art director of Linshaobin Design Studio.

www.linshaobin.com

p.032-033, 046-047, 078, 082-083, 100-101, 176-177

Li Xibin & Yao Ye

Li Xibin and Yao Ye are the co-founders of Shan Design Studio. It's a professional consulting company. They provide design proposals for clients which will combine the art and business perfectly and set up attractive culture and art platforms.

www.s-h-a-n.com

p.173, 222

LonBrand

Alon is the creative director and manager of Shanghai LonBrand. With 16 years' experiences in advertising design, he serves for China Telecom, Pepsi, Citibank, Wanke Real Estate ect. He won many advertising awards all over the world.

www.lonbrand.com

p.170-171

Manual

Manual is a San Francisco based design studio focusing on identity, print, packaging and interactive design with clients in fashion, technology, art, design, and architecture. Manual also curates and publishes Loose Leaf – a large format printed art publication designed to hang on a wall.

www.manualcreative.com

p.040-041, 145

Marc Kandalaft Design

In 2000, Marc founds Marc Kandalaft Design in Paris after graduating from ESAG - Penninghen / Académie Julian in Paris.

Seven years later, he starts exploring the North American market and this will take him to Canada where the company is now based.

Marc creates visual identity concepts for companies and brands for which he also develops communication strategies and websites. He is also a photographer and collaborates regularly with other artists on movie, as well as interior and industrial design projects.

He is also a founding member of the group SEPT.

www.marckandalaft.com

p.147

Mash Creative

Mash Creative is an independent design studio based in East London / Essex. We work on creative projects that include identity & branding, print media and web design. In a short space of time we have acquired a reputation for producing innovative and effective graphic design that is engaging, clear and relevant. We don't believe in just one approach, which is why our work is always unique - producing relevant and successful solutions which add value to our clients' brands.

www.mashcreative.co.uk

p.048-051

Miklós Kiss

A Hungarian designer and artist. He was born in Dunaújváros, HU. After graduation from Hungarian Academy of Fine Arts, he worked on projects in architecture, fine arts, design, graphic design and typography.

www.kissmiklos.com

Mind Design

Mind Design is a London-based independent graphic design studio founded by Holger Jacobs in 1999 after graduating from the Royal College of Art. The studio specializes in the development of visual identities and has worked for a wide range of clients in different sectors.

www.minddesign.co.uk

Mirko Ilić Corp

Mirko Ilić Corp. was established in 1995 as a multi-disciplinary studio specializing in graphic design, 3D animation, motion picture titles, and illustration. The studio is especially known for its strong visual concepts. Mirko Ilić Corp. has received awards from various organizations including the Society of Illustrators, the Society of Publication Designers, the Art Directors Club, I.D. Magazine, Print Magazine, HOW magazine, the Society of Newspaper Design, and more.

www.mirkoilicdesign.com

Mucca Design

Mucca Design is an award-winning Manhattan-based multi-disciplinary design firm with a wide range of work including corporate branding and packaging, as well as book design for world-renowned publishing houses, such as Harper Collins, Random House and Rizzoli. Mucca Design's simple, homespun branding philosophy is: "Great brands deserve great branding, bad brands deserve to work with our competition."

www.muccadesign.com

Nike Brand Design

Nike Brand Design is Nike Brand's creative engine. It initials each seasonal campaign concept and transforms them to unique Nike brand experience.

www.nike.com

Onion Design Associates

Onion Design is a multi-disciplinary graphic and web design consulting studio based in Taipei, Taiwan, China. Our work covers brand identity and web development, art direction, motion graphics and printed literature. We love typography, the web, cats and rock music.

www.oniondesign.com.tw

Patrick Lin

Patrick Lin found his passion in typography when he attended Art Center College of Design; his work was published in The Annual of the Type Directors Club, and Print magazine. Form should follow content and function; while keeping this principal in mind on a daily basis, he has a vision of harnessing the power of design to improve the world around us.

Patrick Lin, was born in China. He worked at several world famous advertising agencies including Ground Zero, David & Goliath and Ogilvy. Now he's working at R/GA in New York.

www.fobdesign.us

Pentagram Design

Pentagram is the world's largest independent design consultancy. Founded in 1972, the company has offices in London, New York, Berlin and Austin, Texas. The firm's 16 partners specialize in different areas of graphic design, industrial design and architecture, producing identities, printed materials, environments, products and interactive media for a wide range of international clients.

Domenic Lippa joined Pentagram in 2006. He has developed a worldwide reputation for work in packaging, print, identity design and retail graphics and was Chairman of the Typographic Circle for two years. The recipient of many awards himself he has judged competitions and lectured extensively.

www.pentagram.com

PMKFA

Graphic designer PMKFA now residing in Tokyo after half a decade in Copenhagen and London. His work spans over different disciplines such as music graphics, the fashion industry and three dimensional art installations.

His colourful and not rarely psychadelic work have been created for people such as DC Shoes, Scion/Toyota, Adidas, Sixpack France, DC Shoes, Uniqlo, Nudie jeans, Wesc, Diesel and many many more.

www.pmkfa.com

Point-Blank Design

Point-Blank Design Ltd. was founded by Lawrence Choy in 1996 providing end-to-end design solutions, from brand identity to commercial interior, point-blanking at the problem and offering aesthetic design, but not bound by style preference.

At Point-Blank Design, brand building is a sophisticated matter of structuring visible and intangible elements, then accentuating the functionality and human dimension of a product or service with unsurpassed creativity. In interior design, we apply specific means and materials to distinguish a brand in a design context that delivers clarity and lucidity, all along taking into account the client's needs.

www.pointblank.com.hk

Queenie He

Queenie He is a senior designer at Nike Brand Design. Her work is in the range of campaign art direction, retail experience design and event/exhibition curation. In her personal time, she also creates secret art events.

www.yehenala.net

Raum Mannheim

Raum Mannheim is an office for visual communication. We develop exceptional images and identities. We design and implement the visual presence of our clients through texts, graphics, illustrations and photographs. We love the challenge of understanding and structuring complex subjects and then transcribing them precisely into various media forms. We think comprehensively, but quality for us lies in details. It is not the size of a project that matters, but rather the specific tasks involved and the individual form it takes on – from an unusual idea to an intriguing concept to a distinctive aesthetic expression. These are the projects that excite our imagination and dare our abilities. The courage our clients show through their willingness to move in unknown territories and use innovative forms of communication is rewarded with a unique and unmistakable corporate design. We are also continually extending our own design spectrum through our own art projects.

We want to cross borders – the borders of perception, the usual, the expected. We want to make a mark in the increasingly standardized world of images.

www.raum-mannheim.com

RoAndCo

RoAndCo is a multi-disciplinary design studio devoted to holistic branding that serves a range of fashion, art, and lifestyle clients. Led by award-winning Creative Director Roanne Adams, RoAndCo offers design, image, and branding capabilities across a variety of mediums, from print to moving image. By thoughtfully distilling a client's inspirations, ideas, and motivations, RoAndCo generates fresh, sincere, compelling brand messages that engage and resonate.

www.roandcostudio.com

Ruiyids

From the beginning of establishment, Ruiyids Design Office has been working to build the cutting-edge design concept and a team with the smart perspective both in market and culture.

www.ruiyids.com

Sagmeister Inc

Stefan Sagmeister, a native of Austria, received his MFA from the University of Applied Arts in Vienna and, as a Fulbright Scholar, a master's degree from Pratt Institute in New York.

He has designed visuals for the Rolling Stones, the Talking Heads and Lou Reed. Having been nominated five times for the Grammies he finally won one for the talking Heads boxed set. He also earned won most international design awards.

In 2001 a best selling monograph about his work titled "Sagmeister, Made you Look" was published by Booth-Clibborn editions. Solo shows on Sagmeister Inc's work have been mounted in Zurich, Vienna, New York, Berlin, Tokyo, Osaka, Prague, Cologne and Seoul. He lectures extensively on all continents.

www.pametjenny.be

Salon de Thé

We are a small studio of 2 designers, Rosa Lladó and Roser Cerdà. We are specialized in book and graphic design. As well as publications we also undertake corporate image projects, exhibition graphics and websites. Our policy is to have a close working relationship with our clients. We continuously collaborate with highly specialized professionals to ensure the highest possible standards in all our projects (photographers, production technicians, designers, programmers, papermakers and printers).

We like people who still get excited about a project, an idea. Let's talk...A cup of tea?

www.salondethe.net

SeventhDesign™

SeventhDesign™ is graphic designer based in Buenos Aires, Argentina, creating customized and ambitious solutions for national and international clients for almost 7 years.

With expertise in identity, print, packaging, interactivity and environments, the SeventhDesign™ studio crafts initiatives that integrate multiple disciplines.

Through wide-ranging capabilities and extensive reach, we coordinate programs that address the spectrum of a client's needs from a unified perspective. This work helps facilitate communication between client stakeholders, resulting in adaptable systems that define visual communication across an organization.

www.seventhdesign.com.ar

Studio Intraligi

Studio Intraligi by Philippe Intraligi was founded 10 years ago on the principle of following one's dreams. In that time, he has travelled across the globe, learning from and collaborating with some of the most creative people in the fields of advertising, corporate design and fashion. He worked at MetaDesign and adidas originals in Germany, age. in Brasil, Leagas Delaney in Italy and Li-Ning in China. Based in New York, Philippe has proved himself to be always ready for challenges and creating outstanding ideas and design solutions for his clients.

www.intraligi.com

Studiowill

Founded by Joe Kwan in 2009, Studiowill is a Hong Kong China based design studio. Specialize in print, branding, corporate identity, packaging, environmental graphic, etc. They have great passion for what they do, and always base their projects on knowledge about the client's reality. Hunger for pushing the limits and big heart beating for new challenging creative ideas, Studiowill creates crafted graphic design for open-minded people.

www.studiowill.com

Taku Satoh Design Office Inc

Established in 1984,producing graphic designs, commercial designs, and branding and planning of exhibition etc. Planning and publication of books. Involved in planning and art direction of TV program on kids educational channel.

www.tsdo.co.jp

THERE

THERE is a creative and strategic brand development agency specializing in brand identity in the built environment. Creatively led – yet strategic thinking and production knowledge is their foundation. For over 10 years they have been building bridges between architecture and graphics.

They have developed a reputation for creating powerful, effective, award-winning identities that give their clients a commercial edge. From idea to outcome THERE have been assisting brands shifting from where they are to where they want to be.

www.there.com.au

Thonik

Thonik designs visual communication. What sets Thonik apart from the rest is its clear design idiom coupled with a focus on content. The firm unites a conceptual design method with an emphasis on typography. Thonik has gradually introduced this graphic language and method into multimedia campaigns for major clients. Strategies originally developed for brands and markets are being applied in surprising ways in a non-commercial context. The strength and confidence of Thonik's work and its experimental character make it instantly recognizable.

Recent clients; Museum Boijmans van Beuningen, Venice Architecture Biennale (2008), Dutch Socialist Party (SP) and the Amsterdam Public Library.

www.thonik.nl

Toormix

Toormix is a Barcelona-based design studio specializing in branding, art direction, creativity and graphic design, set up in 2000 by Ferran Mitjans and Oriol Armengou. We carry out corporate identity, editorial, print, web and communication projects for a wide variety of clients, from small graphic pieces to global branding and communication projects.

Our way of working is based around strategic collaboration with the client. Starting from information and ideas, we develop a clear and coherent creative discourse in order to reach people through innovative and visually attractive design proposals.

At Toormix we play with brands, because playing means not being afraid, always going that bit further, taking on new challenges, questioning approaches, and blazing new paths.

www.toormix.com

Truly Deeply

We are obsessive about creating brands that evoke powerful emotional connections with customers.

We unlock the magic of creating outstanding brand expressions that are born out of deep strategic insights, communicating on brand and on message. This seamless process reveals our creatives to be strategic brand thinkers, as well as masters of their creative craft. We succeed only when your brand "truly deeply" connects with your customers and if that requires adding a little "madness" to the equation, then we're up for that as well. We deliver the most powerful and compelling brand platforms, distilling organisational conversations, market immersion and research into telling insight. We thrive on intellect, rigor and a collaborative approach to deliver a commanding brand strategy. We speak and see the world in the language of brand.

We are Truly Deeply.

www.trulydeeply.com.au

p.124-125

Turnstyle

Turnstyle is a graphic design and branding firm founded on the belief that in a crowded marketplace, people gravitate emotionally toward companies and products that project a distinctive style. Design's power is in its ability to craft that stylistic distinction and to communicate on an emotional, visceral level. We emphasize design execution because that's where the analytical rubber meets the emotional road. In a nutshell, we try to breathe life into products and businesses by infusing clever thinking into impeccably executed branded materials.

www.turnstylestudio.com

p.074-075,210-211

TYMOTE

A creative team that centers around graphic design and produces art works for video pictures, computer graphics, music, interface designing, web designing, and etc. The members are Q Asaba, Kent Iitaka, Rei Ishii, Kota Iguchi, Akiou Kato, Satoshi Murai, Hitoshi Morita, Takahiro Yamaguchi. To seek after a high level work, ideas, and project planning, we break down and reconstruct the project by analyzing it from multiple perspectives within members.

www.tymote.jp

p.131, 218-219

Unreal

BAGGING SMASHING DESIGN doesn't always mean putting up with snotty posers sporting pointy hair-dos. Nor should it feel like having your wallet emptied by an oik in a hoodie.

At unreal we think cracking work stems from cracking relationships, so we smile, we chortle and we tickle the brain-cells of staff and clients alike guaranteeing everyone involved comes away with a corking great grin – and more than enough change for the bus home.

www.unreal-uk.com

p.024-025

VBN

VBN is a vivid and innovative design company. Its professional fields unite graphic design, environment consideration, products development, multimedia and other areas of work under one platform. VBN always provides well-rounded solutions for the brand designing, with its main focus upon innovation and experience.

www.vbn.hk

p.086-087, 096-097, 102-103, 122-123

Zhang Lin

Zhang Lin is a creative designer in China. He graduated from Luxun Academy of Fine Arts. He is a member of ICOGRADA and CCII. He established his own studio - Art Inspiration Design Consultant in 2007.

www.yslgart.com

p.180-181, 240-241

ACKNOWLEDGE-
MENTS

We would like to acknowledge our gratitude to the artists and designers for their generous contributions of images, ideas and concepts. We are very grateful to many other people whose names do not appear on the credits but who provided assistance and support. Thanks also go to people who have worked hard on the book and put ungrudging efforts into it. Without you all, the creation and ongoing development of this book would not have been possible and thank you for sharing your innovation and creativity with all our readers.